SPIRITUAL DISCOVERY SERIES

PARENTING: The Early Years

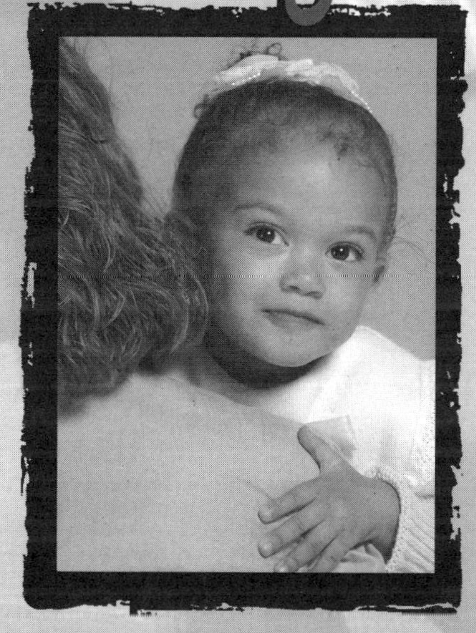

Kay E. Marchand

Radiant Life
1445 Boonville Avenue
Springfield, MO 65802-1894
02-0106

STAFF

National Director: David J. Torgerson
Editor in Chief: Gary Leggett
Series Editor: Clancy Hayes
Assistant Editor: Lori Horne
Assistant Editor: Gerald Parks
Editorial Assistant: Terry L. Bryant
Design Director: Steve Lopez
Assistant Design Director: Marilyn Jansen

Photo Credits:
© 1995 PhotoDisc, Inc,: Cover.; Chris Rockafellow, Rockafellow Photography: Cover, 19; Mark Wright, Rockafellow Photography: 38, 45, 47, 67; Charlie Borland: 12, 22, 35; Bryan Peterson, Charlie Borland Photography: 59; Cleo Photography: 52; Rick Davis: 26, 70; Donna Meier: 15; Karen Mullin: 54, 73; Paul Pavilk: 41; Skjold Photographs: 7; Jim Whitmer Photography: 30, 63, 76.

Springfield, Missouri 65802-1894

Library Of Congress Catalog Card Number 95-77707
ISBN 0-88243-106-4
Printed in the United States of America

A Leader's Guide for individual or group study with this book is available (order number 02-0206). ISBN: 0-88243-206-0

Contents

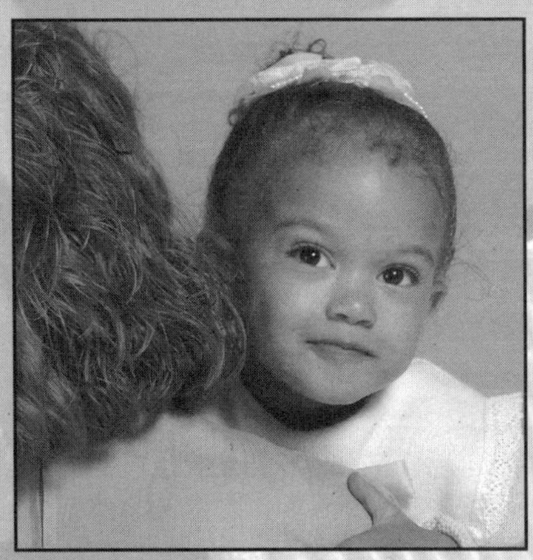

Welcome To The Spiritual Discovery Series

We are glad you have chosen to study with us. We believe the discoveries you make through the use of the *Spiritual Discovery Series* will positively impact your life.

The *Spiritual Discovery Series* will challenge the user to ask questions of the biblical text, discover principles from the text, and make personal application of those truths. The Bible is the text. This guide is a tool for study.

The *Spiritual Discovery Series* is designed for use in either individual or group settings. Individuals will be excited by the discoveries made possible through a structured inductive study. Sunday School classes and other groups will find the *Spiritual Discovery Series* a valuable tool for promoting enlightened discussions centered on biblical truth.

How To Use This Study Guide

1 Pray before beginning each study session. Ask the Holy Spirit to illuminate your mind.

---

2 Choose a translation of the Bible which you trust and can understand. It will be helpful to have more than one translation available to aid your understanding of the biblical text.

---

3 The Bible is your primary text. Avoid using commentaries or reference books until after completing your own study. Reference works are best used to confirm your findings. On occasion, the study guide will direct you to use reference material. This is done when special insights are necessary for proper interpretation.

---

4 Read the assigned biblical text at least twice before answering any questions. This will provide an overview and focus on God's Word.

---

5 Concentrate on the biblical passage which you are studying. It is tempting to jump from one passage of Scripture to another in an attempt to make spiritual connections.

---

6 Seek tangible ways to apply the principles gleaned from each study. Bible study should never result in "head knowledge" alone. Bible study should lead to action.

STUDY 1

PREPARING FOR YOUR NEWBORN

Children stretch the emotions and resources of parents. At times, the parent-child relationship provides feelings of satisfaction, pride, and joy. At other times, the parent-child relationship results in feelings of frustration and inadequacy.

Fortunately, God has provided various resources to enable parents to be effective. Most importantly, He has given us direction and guidance through His Word. God expects parents to use all the resources He has made available in preparation for these challenges.

PRELIMINARY CONSIDERATIONS

The discovery that a new family member is on the way triggers a flurry of activities. Preparations must be made to greet the new arrival. A high priority must be placed on preparing the child's physical environment.

Sleeping occupies the majority of the newborn's time. A baby may sleep from 12 to 20 hours a day the first few weeks, so a good place to sleep is a must. Either a crib or a bassinet with a firm mattress provide a suitable resting place.

The child should sleep in a room of its own if possible. Most parents find they and the baby sleep better if the child is not in the parents' bedroom. Soundproofing the sleeping area is not necessary. The infant needs to learn to sleep through normal household noises. Be sure the room is free of drafts which can chill the baby. This precaution is important in summer as well as winter months.

1. How does establishing and maintaining our homes today compare with homes in Bible times? (Proverbs 31:13-27).

Another decision to be made before the baby's arrival concerns feeding. God provided the best-suited food available through breast milk. But formula feeding can also be nutritious and satisfying. Expectant mothers (and fathers, too!) should consult their physician and read available literature regarding nursing and formula feeding. Parents should make an informed, guilt-free decision.

Occasionally parents prop bottles on pillows or other objects so the infant can eat while the parent carries on other activities. This should be avoided for a variety of reasons. Propping a bottle can lead to physical problems such as ear infections, tooth decay, and stomach upsets. Propping a bottle also robs the parent and child of important emotional interaction. Cuddling, talking, and eye contact baby receives during mealtime is as important as the nutrition itself. Bonding—the development of lifelong emotional attachment—can be enhanced during feedings. Parents who interact with their infant during the feeding process will have memories which will be treasured in the years to come. Memories such as these may have helped sustain Mary, the mother of Jesus, during the pain of His crucifixion.

2. How can good memories help parents deal with various difficulties (illness, rebellion, etc.) that may arise? (Luke 2:19).

Another major decision involves child care. Many parents agree it would be desirable for the child to stay home with a loving parent for the first few years. Unfortunately, societal conditions make this difficult, if not impossible. Many couples believe they need two incomes to get by, and most single parents have to work outside the home.

Some couples make the necessary sacrifice in lifestyle so Mom or Dad can stay home with the baby. Many feel a full-time parent provides the most advantages for the child, and the whole family.

3. **What advantages and disadvantages do you see in having one parent stay home with the child(ren)?**

___

___

4. **What sacrifices would you have to make for one parent to stay home with the children? Would the advantages be worth the cost?**

___

___

In other cases, decisions are made to find child care. Options for child care may include family members, neighbors, those who provide care in their homes, caregivers who come to your home, and day-care centers. Each option has its own advantages and disadvantages. A list of prospects can be found through other parents, local physicians, clinics, the telephone directory, and the newspaper. Also, area churches may recommend individuals or groups that provide quality care.

Your primary concern as a parent is to provide for your child's safety and well-being. The caregiver you select needs to supply a loving environment to stimulate the child's growth and development. The caregiver's philosophies on child care need to agree with your own.

Selecting a caregiver is an important responsibility. Interview prospective caregivers and visit their facilities. Don't hesitate to ask questions pertinent to the children in their care. Insist on references. During your visit, observe other children in their care. Are they happy and involved in interesting age-related activities? Is needed discipline handled in a loving yet firm manner? Is the facility clean, attractive, and geared to the care of children? Drop in for an unannounced visit. If your unexpected visit causes concern or alarm, consider this as a red flag and continue your search elsewhere. Parents should always be welcome, whether in a day-care center or a private home.

5. **List three child care facilities/options available to you in your area.**

___

___

___

___

Christian parents must not overlook the importance of prayer in preparing for a child. Prayer, both as a couple and individually, should be a high priority. Prayer offers access to the greatest resource for parenting and family life, God. It also provides the model for the child to follow.

Prayer gives parents opportunity to hear from God when disagreements occur. Prayer allows God to give guidance in all situations, and encourages parents to listen. Prayer is an important key in establishing unity between parents which will strengthen the family unit.

6. What things seem to undermine your efforts at prayer?

Caring for a newborn requires many schedule adjustments and personal flexibility. It is common for parents to be busy with their new baby and neglect portions of their daily routine. They may find that the dishes, cooking, and cleaning are neglected as a result of caring for the baby. Sometimes even the things of God are neglected. It may seem there is no time or energy for prayer.

7. What is the danger of becoming too busy to pray?

It may be hard to find a regular prayer time for yourself or as a family. However, you should purpose to schedule time for prayer. The secret to obtaining strength to do the seemingly impossible can be found during times of communing with God. Parental burnout can be avoided by spending time in God's presence.

When the baby first arrives, you may think it is impossible to find a consistent time to pray. Don't become discouraged, in about 6 weeks the baby should have developed a regular schedule. This should help you schedule regular times in the Word and prayer.

PERSONAL PREPARATION

Current conditions are much different from those faced by our parents when we were born. Few of us have the advantage of living near our parents, grandparents, or other members of our extended families. Information concerning parenting skills, which used to be passed from generation to generation, now must be obtained by some other source.

Fortunately, resources are available today that our parents and grandparents never imagined. These helps can be beneficial in facing the challenges of parenting. A survey of the local library or bookstore will reveal many magazines, books, and videos, both secular and Christian, which address the subject of parenting. Another good source of information is the family physician.

It is important to consider the philosophy behind the information you obtain. As a Christian parent, you will want your parenting practices to reflect biblical truth. Materials endorsing an extreme view, whether permissive or authoritarian, should be viewed critically. God combines love and mercy with justice as He deals with His children. Should you do any less?

8. According to Proverbs 4:1-7, what should be the primary goal of parenting?

---

9. What can you do as a parent to make this goal a reality?

Many expectant parents need information regarding the actual delivery of the child. Most communities offer classes. These classes are usually offered by hospitals and organizations committed to natural childbirth. Couples learn what to expect during pregnancy and childbirth. Both parents are encouraged to participate in the actual birthing experience. These classes are designed to reduce the fears associated with childbirth. Minimizing fear allows expectant parents to focus on the miracle of life.

10. List questions or fears you have regarding the birth of your child.

Communication is an important ingredient in marriage and essential for parenthood. Couples need to compare their ideas and expectations regarding parenting. Since couples grow up in different homes, they hold different ideas regarding the role of father and mother. Many decisions should be made. Will the father change diapers? Will the mother participate in the discipline of the child? What types of discipline should be used? A great deal of anxiety and hurt feelings can be avoided if roles are clearly understood before the child arrives.

Couples need to discuss their childhood, how they were raised, and the memories they have of growing up. They should compare their expectations regarding parental roles. Both parents need to be willing to compromise to make things work in the family. All families are unique, with their own set of circumstances. What worked for one's parents will not necessarily be the right answer for the new family unit.

Husbands and wives should be in agreement to do whatever is best for their family. The unity that results will benefit the entire family.

11. According to Amos 3:3, why is it important to discuss matters regarding parenting responsibilities?

---

12. Set a time to speak to your spouse regarding the matter of parental responsibilities. If you are a single parent, set a time when you can think through your responsibilities and determine ways others may assist you. Record the appointment time and date below.

God expects us to prepare ourselves for the responsibility of parenting but preparation alone is not enough. We must seek our ultimate strength from God.

Thankfully, God does not leave us to fend for ourselves. He is vitally concerned about the success of our families.

God knows how difficult it is to raise a family in our complex world. He knows the daily struggles and challenges that are faced. God invites us to look to Him. We can avoid many frustrations if we seek God daily for strength, wisdom, and guidance. Spiritual preparation is essential for accomplishing the tasks involved in successful Christian parenting.

13. How does God's invitation recorded in James 1:5 provide encouragement to you as a parent?

____

____

PREPARING OTHER FAMILY MEMBERS

If the child you are about to have is not your first, you will soon become aware that others will be affected by the arrival of the new child. A foreigner will soon invade the secure environment of the home. Suddenly, things will have to be shared—toys, perhaps a bedroom, Mama's lap. Just who does this newcomer think he is, anyway?

It is the parents' responsibility to ease the adjustment for all involved. Healthy sibling relationships seldom occur on their own. Parents must purpose to foster the sibling relationship even before the new baby arrives.

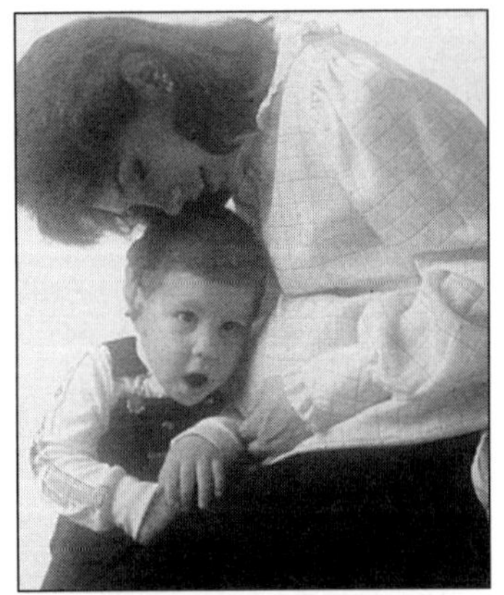

There are a number of things you can do to enhance the possibility of a healthy sibling relationship. For starters, involve the older child in preparing for the new baby. Include the older child in discussions about fixing up the nursery or buying clothing and toys. Avoid making the older child feel like he is being displaced in favor of the new baby. If the older child is still using the crib you need for the new baby, consider moving the older child to a different bed before the new baby arrives. Put the old crib away in storage. As the time draws near to prepare the room for the baby, the older child won't feel like something of his is being taken away. The older child may even suggest "letting the new baby have my old crib." That way he feels like part of the solution, not the problem.

Another way to prepare the older child is by giving him some "privileges of ownership" regarding the new baby. The baby should not be off-limits to the older sibling. The older child should be allowed to touch, kiss, and interact with the baby. If the older child is admonished, "Don't hurt the baby!" "Don't cough on the baby!" "Don't wake the baby!" the child may feel like he can do nothing right. A natural reaction is resentment on the part of the older child. It is important to evaluate our "don't" list and keep it to a minimum. Both children will benefit from interaction.

Another important thing to remember is to keep communication open with all your children. Explain why babies act as they do, and why they need so much attention. Assure them you understand their feelings, and set aside special time to listen to their concerns. Sibling rivalry often occurs because one of the children feels unloved.

14. Read Genesis 25:21-28. What conditions in that home may have contributed to Esau and Jacob's relationship?

Extended family members will also be affected by the birth of a child. Grandparents may regard the event with mixed feelings, but excitement usually tops the list. Being a grandparent can be a rewarding experience. Some feel it is a reward for having been a parent!

As well as enjoyment, there is also responsibility as a grandparent. The influence a grandparent can have in a child's life is second only to the parent. Ideally, parents and grandparents are of like mind concerning faith and family. When the same messages are received from both sources, it increases the likelihood the child will accept those teachings.

Parents can help grandparents prepare for their new role by keeping communication open. Let the new grandparents know their input is welcome and their suggestions will be prayerfully considered. However, it may be necessary to tactfully convey the responsibility for final decisions on raising the child is the parents'.

There is a lot to be gained from listening to godly parents. They have already dealt with most, if not all, circumstances this generation faces. Even though specific situations may be different, human nature isn't. A grandparent's wisdom should be valued. Remember, most grandparents care deeply about the welfare of your child.

Enlist grandparents to pray regularly for you and your child. Impress upon them the importance of intercession. Only eternity will reveal the number of people protected and influenced for Christ as a direct result of a grandparent's prayer.

15. Read 2 Timothy 1:5. What impact did Timothy's mother and grandmother have on his faith?

---

16. How might you replicate your faith in your offspring?

SUMMARY

Parenting is an awesome responsibility. Fortunately, many resources exist to help us with this task. It is our responsibility to avail ourselves of the informational, relational, and spiritual resources which are readily available.

LET'S REVIEW

1. What are some practical steps we can take to prepare for parenthood?

2. Why is prayer such an important part of a young family's life?

3. How can parents agree on the various roles each will fill in the family?

4. How can older siblings be helped in adjusting to the birth of a new baby?

5. What roles can new grandparents fill?

STUDY 2

THE FIRST MONTHS

The first months following the birth of a child are filled with new developments and major adjustments for every member of the family. Sleep patterns well established over the years are often disturbed by a cry in the night. Life, which once centered around your needs and desires, now centers on the needs and desires of your child.

Not all the changes will not be inconveniences. Your home will be enriched by your child's first smile, the gentle sounds of a baby's coo, and the joy of holding your baby close.

The changes which occur in these first months are God's way of developing both parent and child.

DEVELOPMENTAL CHANGES

Candidly, most babies would not win a beauty pageant when first born. The body is not proportioned. With a nearly nonexistent neck and bulging abdomen, sometimes misshaped head, narrow shoulders, flattened nose, and a receded chin, babies can look rather comical. Yet these same features are precious to new parents.

1. Read Psalm 139:13-16. How does the sight of a new life reinforce your belief in the reality of God?

A common question asked by prospective parents concerns the capabilities of a newborn. It is interesting to note the stages of the baby's development as he grows physically, emotionally, socially, mentally, and spiritually.

Let's first look at the physical development of the child.

At birth, a baby's vision is limited. Bright colors are more noticeable than pastels. For the first few weeks, the baby's range of vision is from 8 to 12 inches. It is interesting that this is the approximate distance from the newborn's face to his mother's or father's eyes when he is being held. Vision improves rapidly. In the fourth month, a baby's vision is almost as good as a young adult's.

2. What advantages do you see in a newborn's narrow range of vision?

A newborn's hearing is quite good at the time of birth. The sense of hearing is one the baby practiced while still in the womb.

The senses of taste and smell are less developed. However, it only takes a few days for them to become more sensitive. A 10-day-old baby responds to his mother more on the basis of smell than sight or sound.

Newborns react to touch immediately. A gentle touch may be very calming, whereas a more sudden touch may elicit a startled response.

Newborns have three primary instinctive responses. The rooting reflex, the grasping reflex, and the startle reflex. The child does not willfully produce these actions, they are built-in responses to external stimuli.

The rooting reflex is of particular importance. Whenever the child feels something brush against his lips or cheek, he will turn to it and try to suck.

The grasping reflex is quite interesting. The baby will automatically grab onto anything that touches his palm. His grasp is so strong that he could actually support his own weight. However, since he will turn loose without warning, it is best not to experiment!

The startle reflex is a reaction to a sudden loud noise or abrupt touch to the abdominal area. The baby cries and extends his arms and legs.

Interestingly, each of these reflexes will disappear as a learned behavior takes its place.

✎ **3. How do each of these instincts aid in a child's survival?**

____

____

____

____

Emotional development is noticed as the child learns to express feelings. The first emotion a child will display is excitement. Even newborns can exhibit this response. Within the first few months, the child will also show the emotions of fear, pleasure, anger, and joy. At about 9 months of age, the child becomes capable of expressing affection. That first hug (with sticky hands!) and kiss (guaranteed to be wet!) are milestones treasured by parents.

✎ **4. Read Luke 1:41-44. What does this passage demonstrate about a child's emotional capabilities even before birth?**

____

____

____

____

Social interaction begins almost immediately. The infant's total dependency forces him to interact with others in order to fulfill his needs.

Evidence of social development is seen as the baby responds to the people around him. At 4 to 6 weeks the child's face lights up as his mother or father approaches. At about 6 months the baby wants to play interactive games such as "pat-a-cake" and "peek-a-boo."

It is important to understand that a baby is egocentric. The baby believes the world exists to bring him pleasure and satisfaction. The process of socialization will eventually help him become more aware of the needs of others. Don't expect this to happen overnight. Socialization is one of the more difficult developmental tasks encountered. Most adults continue to battle self-centeredness throughout life.

✎ **5. How can knowing the normal stages and patterns of child social development benefit parents?**

____

____

____

____

Intellectually, newborn children might be compared to a sponge waiting to be saturated. Newborns use all of their senses to gather information from their environment. Intellectual growth occurs rapidly in infants. A great amount of experiential knowledge is gained within the first few months.

One critical development in the area of intellect is "object permanence." At about 9 or 10 months the child learns that things continue to exist even when they are out-of-sight. Prior to this, the child assumes things (including people) become nonexistent when they vanish from sight. When object permanence occurs, the child begins to show signs of curiosity about things happening outside his vision. He now knows he might be missing an interesting activity in another room. He also knows to look for lost toys or forbidden objects.

Increased memory and the concept of object permanence help the child to problem solve. The out-of-reach toy, the cabinet that won't quite open, and the stairs that are blocked, may provide challenges the baby will try to solve.

Learning is enhanced by routine. The child learns to associate being bathed, dressed in pajamas, and listening to a story with bedtime. He hears a car in the driveway and anticipates company. He sees his parent using the phone and knows now is his chance to check out that cabinet that is off-limits.

The child learns from interaction with others. He discovers which actions get positive feedback and which actions get negative feedback. He learns through his senses and from his experiences.

6. Compare a newborn child with a 1-year-old child. What differences do you see in the area of intellect? How is this instructive regarding your responsibility to your child in the first year of life?

____

____

____

____

The child is spiritually receptive at an early age. In the early months, prayer time, Bible stories, and Bible/Christian songs should be a regular part of the child's environment. This prepares the child to understand his need to accept Christ as Savior as he grows older. Early modeling on the part of parents will provide a foundation for further spiritual development.

7. What benefits await a child who is provided a godly pattern and chooses to follow it? (Proverbs 3:1-4).

____

____

____

It is a privilege to see God's handiwork in the lives of our children as they grow, develop, and mature. It is our responsibility to provide them with a warm, loving environment with lots of communication and interaction to stimulate their continual growth.

PERSONAL ADJUSTMENTS

All Christian parents hope their children will become happy, well-adjusted, God-fearing young adults. This isn't likely to happen without a concerted effort on the part of the parents. Successful children most often result from interested and involved parents.

Personal sacrifice is an important aspect of parenting. Parents have to put many of their own needs, wants, and even dreams on hold while they care for the needs of their infant child. This sacrifice is a must—it is not optional. Although some may see this type of sacrifice as an undue burden, most will accept it as an act of love offered to their newborn child.

8. According to Psalm 127:3-5, what attitude should Christian parents have toward their child?

____

____

____

Building trust and establishing security in our children is vital. Our children need to know they can count on us to take care of them, give love, and provide protection.

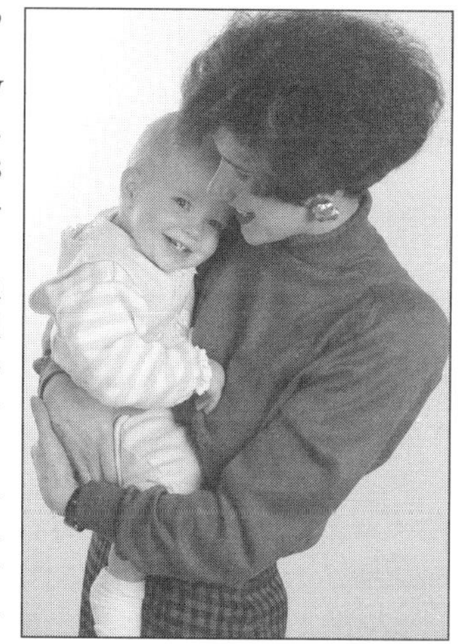

In the early months, trust is established by meeting the child's needs as the needs occur. When the child is hungry, we feed him. If he is wet, we change him. If frightened, we try to comfort him.

Some people are afraid that attending to an infant's need on demand will spoil him, and encourage demanding behavior. Not so! We merely show the child we are there for him, and reinforce his trust.

Do you remember how, early in your Christian walk, God tenderly cared for you? Each time you prayed, an answer quickly came. God firmly established in your heart that He was there for you and could be trusted. Only after that trust was well established did God begin to teach you necessary lessons in patience and waiting. God's treatment of His children should encourage you as a parent.

9. Read 2 Chronicles 26:4,5. Why did the son follow in the steps of his father? What responsibility does this place on Christian parents?

____

____

____

____

Another major adjustment for mothers regards their emotions. A common malady, sometimes referred to as "baby-blues," occurs in the weeks and sometimes months following the baby's delivery. "Baby-blues" or postpartum depression results from hormonal fluctuation as the mother's body readjusts to a non-pregnant state. Other factors involved in postpartum depression include the mental/emotional adjustment necessitated by the new responsibilities of motherhood.

Mothers often don't understand these feelings of depression, and aren't prepared for them. They wonder why they feel depressed after giving birth to such a beautiful new child. They may feel guilt which will only aggravate the depression and intensify the negative feelings.

Moms and dads need to realize these feelings of depression are normal physical and emotional readjustments. They will go away with time. Mothers need to realize they are not the cause of the problem and shouldn't feel guilty. Deal with the depression by talking about it and praying about it. Dads and other family members can help by being supportive and understanding.

10. Read 2 Corinthians 1:3-7. What encouragement can you glean from these verses during your time of suffering/depression?

SUMMARY

Children are in a constant state of change which demands adjustments on the part of parents. Being knowledgeable about the various developmental phases faced by children during the early months of life can help smooth the transitions. Adjustment to the new lifestyle takes time and energy, but God will be faithful if we will continually look to Him for wisdom and strength.

LET'S REVIEW

1. Why is it important for parents to be aware of developmental stages their child will go through?

2. What physical changes can parents expect to observe in their child during the first few months?

3. What is "object permanence" and how does it affect a child when achieved?

4. How is trust first established in a parent/child relationship?

5. Why do some mothers experience depression after childbirth?

STUDY 3

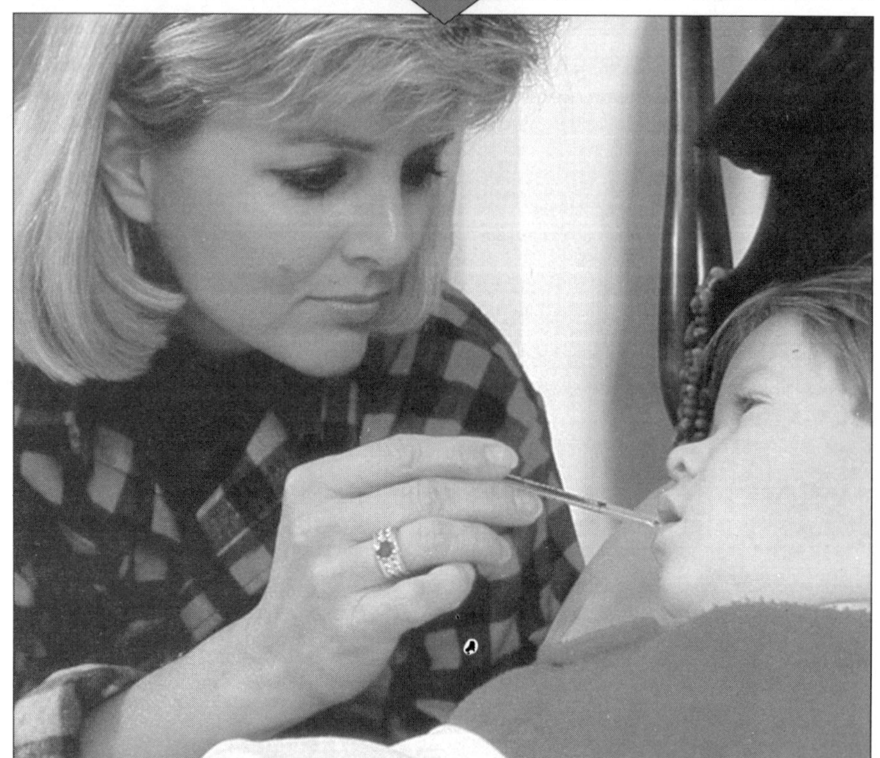

CARING FOR YOUR CHILD

What do new toasters, cars, washing machines, and a bottle of aspirin have in common? They all come with instructions! But new babies? They come with a lot of needs and wants, but no instructions. Sorry!

Ironic, isn't it? The most important job any of us could ever face comes without directions. We're told how to make a perfect slice of toast, but not how to raise "perfect" children!

But there is hope and help. As we saw in the previous studies, a lot of information is available to help us. God did not leave us alone in this endeavor. He has provided guidance and direction through His Word and His people.

CARING FOR PHYSICAL NEEDS

Children's most obvious needs are physical in nature. This isn't to say these are the most important needs—they are simply the most visible.

One basic need of a child is proper nutrition. At first, either breast milk or formula is required. Somewhere between 4 and 6 months, the baby will be ready for "solid" foods.

In the natural progression you begin with rice cereal (few are allergic to this) mixed to a thin consistency with either formula or breast milk. Gradually other foods are added at the rate of one per week. Begin by adding other cereals, then vegetables, fruits, and finally meats. Either purchase prepared, strained baby foods, or make your own using a blender or food processor. Make sure the food has no additives like salt, sugar, or preservatives. Those things are added to food to appeal to adult taste buds, not for a baby's. The child won't miss what he never had. Plus, you won't contribute to the development of a sweet tooth!

Always transfer the food from the jar to a dish. If the baby is fed directly from the jar, saliva is introduced from the baby's mouth to the jar. If leftover food is served later, the bacteria in the saliva will have grown (even with refrigeration) into something that could make the child ill. It is better to be safe than sorry! Also, serving from a bowl avoids the slight possibility of the child ingesting glass which may have chipped from the jar.

Serve balanced meals and snacks, using a variety of foods from the basic food groups. The child will learn to like what you serve. A child will learn to like whole grain crackers and fruit for snacks, rather than cookies or sweetened drinks, if that is what you serve.

What if the baby doesn't like a new food? Chances are, it is not a true dislike, but a reaction to a new experience. Put that food aside for a couple weeks, then try again. Never force a child to eat something. It is a battle you may win but it is not worth the long-range effects.

1. What are some foods which you did not like as a child which you later acquired a taste for?

____

____

Keeping mealtime pleasant should be a top priority. Mealtime provides an opportunity for a pleasant exchange between parent and child. This interaction is an important ingredient in healthy relationships.

A newborn must be fed on demand. When he is hungry he is in great discomfort and making him wait serves no purpose. You can direct him to a workable schedule over a period of time. Don't encourage a baby to eat more than he wants.

When the child begins eating solids, mealtime patterns begin to emerge. By the time he is 3 years of age, the child should eat what the rest of the family eats.

Whereas a set timetable for meals is ill-advised for a newborn, allowing an older child to set his own mealtime schedule is equally unwise. Allowing the child to eat anytime he wishes often restricts his hunger at mealtime. He then becomes hungry before the next mealtime. This vicious cycle can be avoided by learning to say no at the appropriate time. It will be in the best interest of all involved to teach the toddler to eat according to the family schedule.

2. Read Matthew 7:9-11. What assumptions does Jesus make regarding a parent's concern for his child?

Medical care is an important part of maintaining a child's health. Regular checkups provide reassurance that all is well and can prevent health problems from developing. Many parents have taken an apparently robust, healthy child in for a regular checkup, only to find a problem in the early stages. Early detection allows prompt treatment that often means a full recovery.

Immunizations are another aspect of regular medical care. There is some controversy about the wisdom in receiving immunizations. Some feel the risks in taking them are too great. Indeed, there have been documented cases of serious reactions to immunizations. However, many lives have been saved because of modern immunizations. Many serious illnesses have been avoided and much pain and suffering have been averted. Most of today's parents grew up when few childhood illnesses were uncontrolled and few serious epidemics were evident. This was not the case prior to widespread immunizations. Immunizations have saved multitudes from serious illnesses such as polio and diphtheria.

3. Read 1 Timothy 5:23. What does this verse teach about the wisdom of utilizing available forms of preventive medicine?

There are some common childhood illnesses for which there are no immunizations.

One illness most children have sooner or later is chicken pox. Caused by a virus, the symptoms include itchy blisters, a fever of 100 to 101 degrees Fahrenheit, a mild headache, and cold symptoms. The worst of the symptoms last 5 to 7 days. Complications are rare.

Another common disease is roseola. Also caused by a virus, roseola has few symptoms other than a high fever (103-104 degrees Fahrenheit). The fever will disappear after a day or two, and the child will feel better and then develop a flat, red rash which covers the body. After 2 or 3 days, the rash clears and the child is fine. No complications are known.

Strep throat and scarlet fever are caused by a bacterial infection. A severe sore throat and high fever usually characterize strep throat. Without antibiotic treatment a headache and vomiting may develop accompanied by a red rash (scarlet fever). The skin may peel and there may be hair loss. Both illnesses are highly curable with antibiotics.

Upper-respiratory infections are the most common of childhood illnesses. These include colds, and infections of the ear, nose, and throat. Earaches are a common malady in young children. These can be extremely painful. Small babies may tug at the ear, be fussy and irritable, and may or may not have a fever. Earaches need to be treated by a physician as soon as possible. Frequent ear infections can result in hearing loss.

Lower-respiratory infections, such as bronchitis and pneumonia, are characterized by a cough and sometimes a fever, chest tightness, or discomfort. Even with these symptoms, only the doctor can accurately diagnose these diseases. Treatment will vary depending on the symptoms. It is important to consult your doctor when these symptoms occur because lower-respiratory infections can be severe.

Knowing when to call the doctor can be difficult, but it is best to consult your doctor anytime you have a question concerning your child's health. The following list of symptoms is not complete, but can provide guidance. Call the doctor if:

- a fever is above 101 degrees Fahrenheit.
- a fever lasts more than a day or two.
- there is a noticeable decrease in urine output.
- there is repeated vomiting or diarrhea.
- the child exhibits listlessness or extreme drowsiness.
- the skin is pale and cool, or flushed and hot.
- breathing difficulties occur.

4. Some religions teach that people should refuse to take their children to doctors or go to one themselves. What do the words of Jesus, recorded in Matthew 9:12, indicate about this position?

____

____

____

5. Some people rely too heavily on doctors, neglecting the privileges associated with their faith. What does James 5:14,15 teach concerning sickness and healing?

____

____

6. Devise a commonsense plan concerning your approach to sickness and the physical care of your child. Record that plan below.

____

____

____

Day or night, weekend or holiday, we always have access to the greatest Physician of all. Nothing is too trivial to bring to God. He understands our fears and concerns for the well-being of our children. Praise God for His wisdom and care!

Another important aspect of child care is rest. Children's minds and bodies need physical rest in order to properly grow and develop.

A major milestone is reached when the baby begins sleeping through the night. Rarely does this occur before 5 or 6 weeks of age. By the third month, the baby should begin to show signs of longer periods of sleep. If the child still isn't sleeping through the night by 5 or 6 months, methods can be utilized to encourage this development. Before implementing any plan, check with your doctor to confirm that the baby no longer needs nighttime feedings.

The first method is to let the child cry it out. When the child awakens, check on him with little fanfare. Assuming all is well, tell the child to go to sleep, reassuring him that you will see him in the morning, and return to bed. Be prepared for a 20- to 30-minute cry (or longer!). If you use this method, don't give in and rescue the "poor baby" (unless you hear him choking, as a few will do after prolonged crying). If he eventually wins, he has learned a valuable lesson: "If I cry long enough and loud enough, I'll get my way." Using this method you will see a decrease in waking and crying by the second or at least the third night. Persistence is the key.

A second method takes a more gradual approach. With this method when the baby cries, check on him. If all is OK, tell him you are going back to bed. He will undoubtedly cry again, so check on him again after 5 minutes. Keep repeating the process and increase the length of time you wait from 5 to 10 or 15 minutes. Sooner or later he will give up, deciding this game isn't very rewarding. Using this method gradually weans him from the habit of waking during the night. Be prepared to continue this routine for several nights.

Some people don't like the first method thinking it will harm the child's trust in his parents. They fear he will feel abandoned and frightened. In most cases, if trust has been established through a healthy parent/child bonding, the likelihood of real harm is small. It is important to choose a method and stick with it. The reward will be worth it.

Naps are another issue. The amount of sleep needed decreases as the child gets older. A child of 4 or 5 months has settled in a routine including morning and afternoon naps. By 12 to 18 months, the need for daytime sleep decreases to one afternoon nap. This pattern will be repeated until age 4 or 5. Each child will be different in his need for sleep. Use your judgment based on your knowledge of your child in deciding whether or not to impose naps.

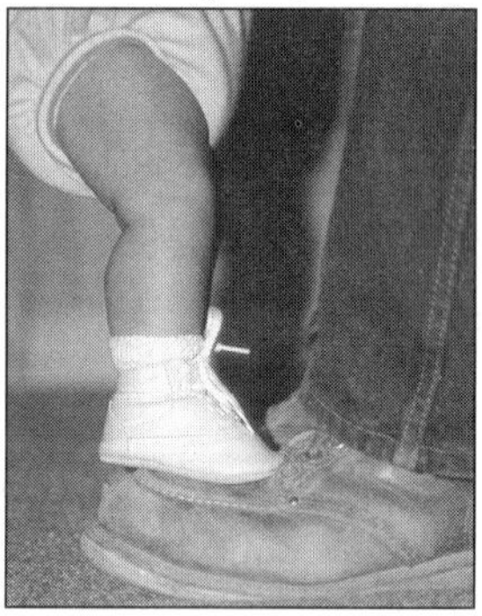

Exercise is important to the developing child. Playing naturally accomplishes this. The climbing, running, crawling, and stretching a child does works all the major muscle groups. Detailed work with the hands such as drawing, cutting, and molding with clay exercise the fine or small muscles of the hands and wrists. Both types of exercise are equally important. Child's play really does more than just entertain and occupy the child. It can legitimately be called the child's "work."

It is up to adults to keep a safe environment. God planted curiosity in children and they naturally explore their surroundings. Babies and toddlers don't have the knowledge to determine if something is harmful. It is up to parents to provide a safe place for them to explore.

Childproofing our homes does not have to be difficult. The best technique is to get down on the child's level and look at each room from his perspective. When possible, remove anything that could be harmful. Lock all cleansers and medications up out of reach. Also, move expensive or cherished breakable items to higher ground. Children don't care about cost or sentiment, they just want to check things out! Use safety covers on electrical outlets and latches on cabinet doors that are off-limits.

✎ **7. Walk through your home making a list of items in your home which could be harmful to a baby.**

____

____

____

Some parents feel a baby or toddler should be taught to leave things alone. This often becomes a struggle of the wills. A child is curious by nature. It is true that a child needs to learn the value of limits, but parents should be careful to limit the number of rules they expect their child to obey. God limited His list to 10. Too many limits become confusing and hard to enforce consistently.

8. Make a list of basic rules which you would expect your child to learn and obey. How do these rules compare to God's rules found in Exodus 20:1-17?

CARING FOR EMOTIONAL NEEDS

Nurturing means to foster growth and development by providing love, support, and encouragement. Nurturing skills stimulate emotional and social growth in the child.

9. Read Isaiah 66:13. What does this passage teach about the importance of nurture? What does it teach about God?

The love between parent and child is unique. It is a one-sided relationship which is sacrificial in nature. The child learns to feel affection for the parent because of the love shown.

10. Read Romans 5:8. How does God's love relationship with His children parallel our relationship with our children?

We demonstrate love to our children in several ways. One is by giving attention to them. Listening, giving sincere answers to their questions, and finding out how they think and feel about things will speak volumes about our love.

Our love must be unconditional. Occasionally, children will do something which does not please us. We must remember children were not given to enhance the life of parents. Conversely, parents are given to children to help them mature and grow. This may mean that a parent must administer discipline but that discipline should never entail withholding love and acceptance.

11. Using Romans 8:38 as a guide, develop a statement of unconditional love to your child.

Children are never too old to hear us say, "I love you." We need to show our love to them by word and deed.

12. Make a list of practical ways you can show love to your children.

Children need encouragement. They need to know when we are proud of them and pleased with what they have done. Far from making them conceited, it prompts them to try for even greater accomplishments.

13. Mark 10:16 shows Jesus taking children in His arms and blessing them. How does a loving touch assist in the communication process?

Providing guidance is one of the most challenging areas of parenting. Guidance helps meet the child's social and behavioral needs. The primary need is to train the child to get along with others. Key skills include teaching the child to take turns and share, to practice proper etiquette, and to respect others and their property. The ultimate goal of the parent is to develop self-discipline in the child.

Discipline provides an avenue for giving guidance. It involves enforcing reasonable limits, modeling desired behaviors, rewarding desired behaviors with praise and encouragement, and appropriate punishment for misbehavior. Consistency in discipline is essential. A lack of consistency will undermine efforts at guidance.

14. According to Proverbs 20:11, why is it important to provide children with proper training and guidance?

SUMMARY

God has entrusted children to the care of parents. Although a mammoth task, parents are given the responsibility of helping children develop physically and emotionally. The job is challenging, but the skills can be learned and developed with the help of God and others.

LET'S REVIEW

✎ 1. Why are immunizations so important?

✎ 2. What four signs should alert parents to take their child to the doctor?

✎ 3. What are two methods for training a child to sleep through the night?

✎ 4. List several practical ways parents can demonstrate unconditional love to their child.

STUDY 4

YOUR CHILD'S FIRST TEACHERS

Say "teacher" and most people envision a classroom complete with books, chalkboard, and recess. However, the child's first and most important teachers don't use a chalkboard or usually give homework. The first and most influential teachers are the child's parents. From the first moments of life, a child learns from the attitude, emotions, and lifestyle of his parents.

God placed parents in a crucial position with immeasurable responsibility. Parents have a wonderful opportunity to influence their children, encourage right decisions, provide direction, and build a foundation that will last a lifetime and beyond.

TEACHING THROUGH DAILY ROUTINE

1. James 3:1 is usually applied to teachers within the church. How can this passage be applied to parenting skills?

One of the pleasures of parenthood is the opportunity to enjoy your child's company. Through daily interaction, you and your child will get to know one another.

2. Deuteronomy 11:18-20 instructs parents to teach their children daily. Why would this ongoing approach be more effective than periodic, structured "lessons"?

Language Skills

A fundamental part of a child's education is language development. Effective communication skills are necessary to further the child's education and to assist him in adequately expressing feelings and ideas.

The best way to teach language skills is to simply talk with your child. From the time of birth, it is important to communicate with your child on a daily basis. Use your child's name. Talk to him about things in his world–his red ball; her soft blanket. Play word games by pointing out your child's nose, hair, toes, fingers, and other body parts. Talk to him about the pretty flowers and busy little puppies. Let your child hear the tenderness in your voice when you tell him you love him and Jesus loves him.

In the early months your baby will not understand what you say, but will respond to the tone of your voice. Words take on meaning through exposure and association.

First your baby will study your face and eyes when you talk to him. Within a few months he will attempt to talk with you. He still doesn't know the words have meaning; it seems to him like a very pleasant game. By 5 or 6 months babies usually try to repeat specific sounds, such as "ba-ba-ba," or "ga-ga-ga." Usually during this time Daddy will hear, "da-da-da" and be positive the baby is saying "daddy." It's not necessary to explain to fathers that babies all begin with hard consonant sounds (g, b, d, for example). The "da-da" sound is, at first, purely accidental.

Talking to and with your child provides many benefits. It enhances the parent-child bonding process. The child learns about the world around him. He also learns sensitivity, compassion, kindness, and concern as he hears them expressed in your voice.

Reading to your child is an extremely healthy interaction that serves as a language builder. Reading encourages the sharing of ideas and the asking of questions, and it gives opportunity to discuss things uncommon to the child. Through reading we nurture the child's emotional development, and stimulate his intellectual progress. If the child grows up with books in his environment, he will likely value books in the future.

The subject matter means little when you are reading to a newborn. It is the tone and voice inflections that interest the infant. As the baby gets older, colorful, durable books with bright, uncluttered pictures are best. Each page should have a simple picture and corresponding word or phrase. Later, the child will prefer books he can relate to and pictures he can identify. By age 2 or 3, the toddler will be ready for simple story lines and plots. Don't insist a story be finished or the pages turned in order. That will come as the child matures and his attention span increases.

Incorporate reading Bible stories early in life. Books with biblical themes or books that reinforce values consistent with the Bible are available for any age level. Ongoing exposure to biblical characters will model godly attitudes and behaviors which the child will hopefully develop throughout the years.

Math And Spatial Concepts

Daily routines help teach basic math and spatial concepts. When we say, "See the two puppies?" we are helping the child learn the meaning of "two." If parents take advantage of opportunities to use words common to counting, size comparisons, distance, or time, they will help their child learn.

It may take some effort to habitually say, "Let's stack three blocks," or "Roll the big ball to me," or "Put the toy under the chair." However, regular exposure of the child to such wording will enrich his learning experiences.

Many parents are thrilled when their 3-year-old can count to 10 or 20. Although an admirable achievement, the child does not understand the concepts behind "1, 2, 3..." and so on. He has merely learned how to repeat the numbers by rote memory. Only through using numbers in everyday situations will the concepts develop.

3. Read Proverbs 4:1-9. As parents, how should this passage affect our teaching methods? Based on this Scripture, what should our goal as parents be for our children?

____

____

____

LIFE/SOCIAL SKILLS

Another area of learning involves skills needed to become fruitful, competent adults. Parents can prepare their children to face the challenges of the future.

A baby begins demonstrating problem-solving skills by 7 or 8 months of age. His thought processes are complex enough to think of different approaches to get what he wants. Many parents have been shocked to find their baby sitting on a counter eating cookies.

Problem solving begins with simple obstacles, like children trying to reach a toy that rolled out of reach. Children continue to develop problem-solving skills throughout life. Older children are demonstrating this skill when they attempt to manipulate adults to get what they want.

Closely related to problem solving is decision making. Babies begin making simple decisions early, such as choosing which toy to reach for, or whether to come when called.

Parents can help their children solve problems and make decisions in several ways. First of all, select toys that stimulate problem solving. Toys that encourage them to figure out how to elicit a particular response (jack-in-the-boxes, pop-up toys), or how to fit parts together (shape sorters, puzzles) are good selections.

Another idea is to offer the child choices. Allow the child to make some decisions based on his level of maturity. Keep the options limited (start with two), and make sure you can accept either choice. A good example would be, "What do you want for breakfast, oatmeal or French toast?" Another would be, "It is chilly outside; do you want your blue jacket or your red sweater?" You still control the situation, yet allow the child to make some decisions. This will prepare him to deal with more serious choices later.

People skills are needed by all. These skills are critical for getting along with others, for exchanging ideas, doing business, and sharing the gospel of Christ.

People skills are best transmitted through parental example. If parents demonstrate respect for others, good listening skills, and good manners, children are likely to develop similar skills. Modeling expected behaviors with explanation, guidance, and consistency should achieve positive results.

4. Read Proverbs 4:1-9 and Acts 1:21-25. What rules or guidelines are found in these Scripture passages that will help us make good decisions?

____

____

____

____

____

5. After reading Romans 8:28 and 2 Corinthians 1:8-10, describe the balance between being self-reliant and counting on God. What role should prayer take in making decisions and solving problems?

____

____

____

____

____

____

SHARING THE CHRISTIAN LIFESTYLE

Some have said example is an excellent teacher. Nowhere is this more true than in parents teaching children about God.

Living The Christian Life

Parents have the unique opportunity of influencing their children to live for Christ. Children know what is important to their parents by what they say and do. How parents spend their time will greatly influence the formation of their children's value system.

6. Psalm 128 has been called the marriage prayer because it was often sung at Israelite weddings. What does this psalm teach regarding devotion to God and family life?

Living the Christian life is an ongoing process. Our children should see us worshiping and praying in and out of church. They should hear us speak of God and His will for our lives. Our children should witness our reliance on God for answers, and hear us give credit to Him when the answers come. They must perceive the Christian faith as a natural component of life.

7. One of the primary ways children learn is through imitation. How can parents apply Titus 2:7,8?

8. What does 1 Thessalonians 5:16-18 say about our attitude in life?

Communing With The Lord

Parents can help their children develop a personal prayer life. Praying with and for our children at bedtime is a good place to start. Even though babies don't understand, they will look forward to the nightly prayers. Encourage them to participate in the prayers as early as possible. Folding hands and bowing heads can demonstrate respect even before they utter their first words. Prayer reinforces the biblical truth that God cares for us and wishes to be a part of our daily lives.

Mealtime is a natural place to model prayers of thanksgiving. Encourage children to take a turn at giving thanks. Use prayer to help them learn God is the source of every good thing.

Our children also need to see us participating in our own personal time of prayer and Bible study. A parent's actions speak volumes to the minds of children. Parents who spend personal time in prayer are investing in the future prayer life of their children.

Relying On God

Parents generally want to appear capable and self-sufficient to their children. This does not mean, however, that parents should avoid demonstrating a reliance on God. It is important to communicate that relying on God is a strength rather than a weakness.

Our children should hear us ask God for guidance and wisdom. When a difficult decision or need is at hand, involve the entire family in seeking God.

It is vital to communicate to our children the wisdom of allowing God to lead us in every area of our lives. If our children see us turning to and following God, they will be inclined to do the same.

9. Often God guides us through problems rather than removing the trouble from our lives. What can we teach our children as we travel through these times of testing (Hebrews 12:12,13)?

____

____

____

GIVING GUIDANCE FOR LEARNING

Many parents ask, "What are some practical ways to help my child learn?" Here are a few basic suggestions which will provide assistance.

Interact often with your child. Show your child how to make cookies and have "tea," grocery shop, and dust the furniture. Give undivided attention to your child by answering questions, listening, and laughing together. Providing a combination of quality and quantity time will stimulate brain activity, which will help develop your child's intellect and understanding of his environment.

Another tip is to be patient and positive. Preschoolers perceive time differently than do adults. Give the child time to think things through and come to conclusions. If a child asks, "Why did my balloon pop?" give him a little information, ask a couple of pertinent questions, then direct the child to the correct answer. Make sure your tone of voice and attitude imply confidence in the child's ability to figure it out. Certainly, it would be easier and faster to just answer the question, but allow the child to participate in the intellectual exercise of figuring it out for himself.

10. Based on Ephesians 6:4, what role does patience play in parenting?

Another suggestion is to give only as much help as is needed. Parents sometimes quickly jump in when their child experiences difficulty. As we control our impulses and allow the child to continue, it will encourage problem solving and perseverance. A good standard is to observe the child's frustration level. If you notice he is becoming frustrated, provide a little help, but let him experience the success of finishing the job himself.

Sometimes it is helpful to demonstrate solutions. The youngster trying to pull a toy through the bars of his crib could be shown how to turn it so it can be extracted. The child who untied his shoes, but can't get them off, may need to be shown how to loosen the strings. This method encourages him to try many approaches in problem solving, and it also teaches him to come to you when he needs help.

Whenever we show our child "how," or explain "why," keep the explanation on his level. Answer his specific questions with short sentences, being sensitive to the child's vocabulary. Ask questions to check his understanding.

11. Deuteronomy 4:9 speaks of learning from the past. Reflect on and record lessons you learned while growing up that will enable you to effectively parent your own children.

SUMMARY

Guiding one's child is a major responsibility of parenthood. Parents are to teach their child practical skills which will transfer to the various situations he will face in life. An essential component of this task is to provide opportunities for the child to make mistakes in a safe and loving environment.

As our child's first teachers, we have the opportunity to help shape his/her future. God designed the home as the primary learning forum. Through daily routine, communication and example, we can positively impact our child for this life and for life eternal.

Parents truly are their children's first and most important teachers. They have a unique opportunity to model their relationship with Christ and influence their children to also serve the Lord.

LET'S REVIEW

1. Give three examples of ways daily routine can be used to teach basic language and math concepts.

2. What is the relationship between problem solving and decision making?

3. How can we help our children become good decision makers?

4. Why are parents' examples so important in teaching their children?

5. Compile a list of ideas that will enhance opportunities for learning.

STUDY 5

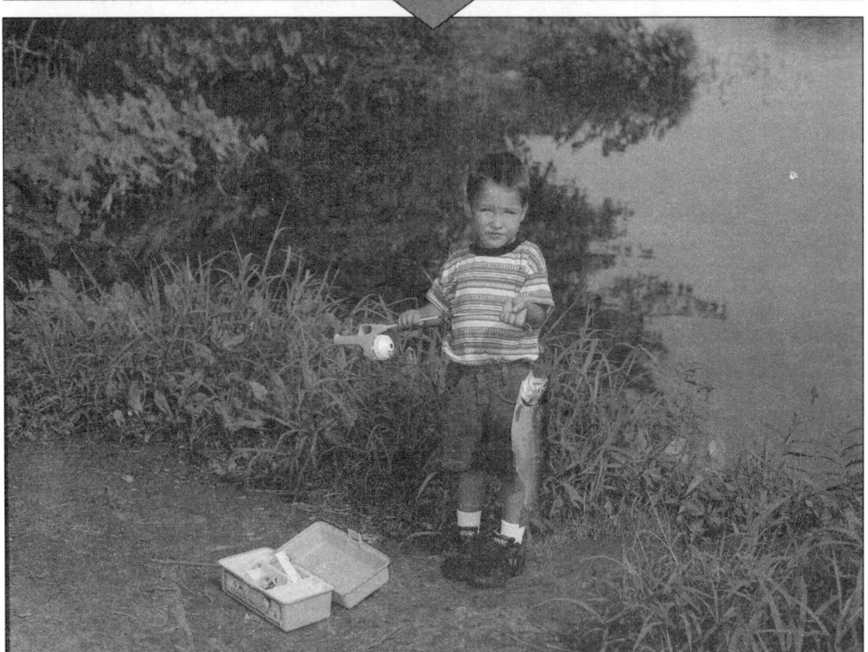

HOW CHILDREN LEARN

The Children's Church leader excitedly told the children about the wonders and beauty of heaven. She concluded her lesson by asking, "Now, who wants to go to heaven?" All the children raised their hands and wildly answered, "I do!" One curly headed 3-year-old piped up, "I want to go to heaven, but I can't today. Mama said we're going to Grandma's after lunch!"

Obviously, children don't interpret information the same way adults do. They seem to approach learning as a natural part of life, rather than a chore. There is something appealing about their curiosity and fascination with the simpler, purer things of life. Over the years, children approach learning in transition. Parents who are aware of the various ways children learn will be ready to help them in the various stages of life.

THE INFANT

All babies act in a similar fashion. They all "speak" the same universal language–they cry. They have the same movements and identical reflexes.

Newborns "know" nothing about social expectations or concrete facts. They can be compared to dry sponges, just waiting to be saturated. Just as a sponge can be soaked with any liquid, from water to kerosene, the child can be filled with different teachings.

1. Consider the intellectual void in each child waiting to be filled. What responsibility does this present to the parent?

____

____

2. Create a list of priorities which you feel are important to instill in the mind and heart of your child.

____

____

____

Newborns have several inborn responses called reflexes. These provide infants with classic responses in their behavior. A very important reflex is the rooting reflex. This will turn babies toward a touch on the cheek or lips, and they will begin a sucking reflex. Another response is the grasp reflex. Babies involuntarily wrap their fingers around anything touching the palm. A third reflex is the startle, or Moro reflex. A sudden touch or noise causes babies to extend their arms and legs. They will look surprised, and they will often cry–loudly.

Another inborn characteristic of the newborn is the tonic neck reflex, or the "fencer's pose." While on his back, the baby usually has his head turned to one side. The arm on the side he is facing stretches out from the shoulder. The other arm is bent at the elbow, with the forearm and hand extended up. This gives the appearance of a dueling swordsman, hence the name "fencer's pose." When the baby turns his head toward the other direction, his arms automatically switch positions.

Learned behaviors will eventually replace each of the reflexes in a newborn. If caregivers know what to watch for, they will observe some interesting changes.

Babies initially learn in two ways. First, their perception distributes information through their senses. Everything they see, hear, touch, taste, and smell is processed through the central nervous system (nerves, spinal cord, and brain). Second, babies learn through experience. Their own actions provide many learning opportunities. Daily routine is an important part of providing the child with consistent learning opportunities.

3. Some children experience an impairment of one or more senses (such as vision or hearing). How would this affect their learning?

____

____

4. What are some ways parents can help children with disabilities compensate to avoid delaying the normal intellectual development process?

___

___

___

Initially, when the newborn sees his mother's face, he doesn't realize what or who she is. Eventually the more he sees her, hears her referred to as "Mama" or "Mother," and observes the roles she fills, he will realize who she is. His experiences, coupled with information from his senses, allow him to learn. This scenario is repeated as he is introduced to new aspects of his environment.

Infants are completely self-centered, or egocentric. This is normal for babies and is nothing to worry about. Babies feel that the world revolves around them. This is a natural assumption when considering the infants' limited view of the world. They don't realize there are other homes where other people exist. Their world is limited to what is being experienced at the moment, at face value. They aren't being selfish, just normal.

Many parents worry their egocentric child will become a selfish adult. This need not be the case. As the child's world expands, he will become aware of others and their needs. As he matures, he will be capable of thinking beyond himself. With the proper guidance, a child will learn appropriate social behavior.

One concept that enhances learning is "object permanence." Initially, the baby does not realize that things–including people–continue to exist even when out of sight. That is why a baby of 3 months won't look for a dropped toy. However, at 5 months the child will look for a toy dropped from the high chair or stroller. But, if the toy is out of sight, he forgets about it. As far as he is concerned, the toy is gone, so he plays with something else.

By 9 or 10 months, the child will actually search for a missing toy, knowing it is there someplace. This represents an important advancement in the child's learning process. Problem solving reflects complex thought processes. In problem solving, the child tries different ways of achieving a goal or resolving a difficulty. For example, if a toy rolls under the crib and the baby can't reach it, he may crawl to the end of the crib and try to get it from there. He may solve some of these problems by getting your attention and help. As exciting as these new developments are, they can cause problems for caregivers. The child is now more creative in getting what he wants, and even learns to manipulate the adults in his world. Parents must be ready to meet these challenges!

5. Some parents make the mistake of interpreting exploration and discovery with sinful rebellion. Read the admonition recorded in 1 Corinthians 14:20. What does this passage indicate about the basic nature of an infant?

___

___

___

___

THE TODDLER

From the time the baby begins to walk until about age 3, he is referred to as a toddler. The toddler stays very busy. He has things to do and places to go. Rarely is he still for more than a moment.

Learning continues at a rapid pace. Memory is maturing to aid his learning process. Evidence of memory shows as early as 8 or 9 months. At this age the child can repeat simple functions such as stacking one block on another, or pulling a string that makes a toy talk. Between 18 months and 2 years the child can repeat 2- and 3-step functions. He may also remember recent events, and mention them if his language skills are adequate.

Without memory, there could be no learning. Memory helps the child recall where he left things, how Dad opened the tool box, where Grandma keeps the cookies, and how to make the jack-in-the-box pop up. He learns that he can depend on his parents. He also learns to sing familiar songs and ask for favorite Bible stories.

The toddler is innately curious. Curiosity, which peaks between ages 8 and 15 months, sometimes gets the toddler into trouble. He doesn't have the maturity to recognize potential danger. It's up to the child's caregivers to watch out for him.

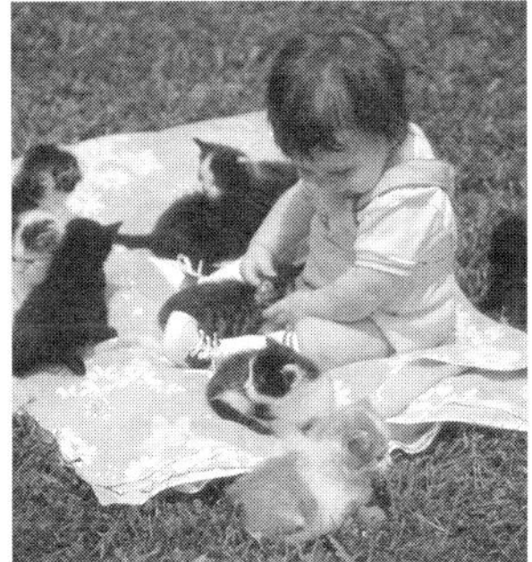

Curiosity is a very important motivator for learning. Curiosity stimulates the child to explore his environment by investigating everything that catches his eye. It is important for parents to provide a safe, secure setting for the child to investigate and to encourage his exploration. Stifling curiosity may lessen the desire to learn, which could have serious lifelong consequences. A child needs to explore, to learn through doing, and to ask "why" and "how."

During the toddler years, the child will learn basic concepts. He will understand and respond to direct commands. The child begins to understand concepts experienced through the senses, such as size relationships, temperatures, textures, and noise levels.

Abstract ideas are not understood by most toddlers. Concepts related to time ("yesterday" or "tomorrow") and to life (plant, animal, and inanimate objects) will take more time and maturity to comprehend.

The toddler still interprets the world around him in light of his own experiences. He is unable to understand or imagine things to which he can't relate. Try to tell a young child who has never seen or touched snow what it is like, and he cannot grasp the idea. This will be true until the early-elementary school years.

The toddler constantly tests what he has learned and the limits set for him. By doing this, the child is making sure there is consistency in both areas. This means parents will be extremely busy keeping up with their child's antics and activities. Caring for a busy toddler requires a lot of patience and wisdom. Understanding the learning process and knowing what is normal and age-appropriate help equip parents to assist their child to grow in the most effective manner.

6. Read 1 Corinthians 13:11. How does this passage reinforce the importance of recognizing age-appropriate behavior throughout life?

7. What dangers exist for parents who hold their children to a standard of behavior which is beyond their child's capabilities?

THE PRESCHOOLER

Toddlers typically blossom into articulate and perceptive preschoolers. Preschoolers are able to carry on complex conversations and express their feelings and ideas. Preschoolers experience fewer frustrations than toddlers and often display a pleasant, sunny disposition.

Preschoolers develop the ability to classify objects. This enables them to organize and process information. Preschoolers notice similarities between dogs and foxes, and between frogs and lizards. They know red, blue, yellow, and green are colors.

By age 3, most children can identify gender. They know whether they are a boy or a girl, and recognize the gender of others. These children recognize Aunt Susan, cousin Mary, and Mama are "girls." They see Dad, Uncle Bob, and Mr. Jones are "boys." This will help them classify relationships. They begin to see the different types of associations among people. They learn what family means, and what friendship means. Also, children begin to recognize the special relationship with their parents.

8. Why is the preschool age an opportune time to introduce children to a relationship with Christ?

Children ages 3 and up have busy imaginations. Until age 5 or so, it is hard for children to differentiate between fact and fantasy. Many children will tell fanciful stories, not to be telling a lie, but as the result of an active imagination. Preschool children often have imaginary friends. They may want you to set a place for their "friend" at lunch or open the door for him. Be assured this is a normal phase of childhood, not a permanent condition. Unless there seems to be an obsession with the "friend," it's not necessary to discourage them. This phase will pass.

9. What is the difference between the child's imagination and fabrication of truth? How should parents handle either situation?

10. Prepackaged "imagination," such as that which is seen on television, often robs a child of the desire to develop his own imagination and creativity. What are some practical ways a parent can help a preschooler foster his imagination and creativity?

The preschooler now has long-term memory. He can remember from one Christmas or birthday to the next, and many memories will last into adulthood. With his improved language skills and memory, he will want to tell others about his experiences. His expanded memory also means he can recall personal limits set by his parents. Although increased conformity to family standards should be expected, it must be remembered that the active child sometimes acts before thinking.

Increased memory means greater retention of biblical teachings. Preschoolers can now grasp truths about the nature of God. Children should be encouraged to view God as a loving Father and turn to Him in prayer with their concerns. Some children do not have a positive father figure. In those cases, it is important to stress the reliability of God and His constant care. It is a privilege to see our children grow in the knowledge of our Lord and build a relationship with Him.

11. How can parents ensure their children develop a good relationship with God?

SUMMARY

It is a wonderful experience and a distinct privilege to watch children develop through the various learning stages. Understanding how intellectual development is accomplished can help parents appreciate and enjoy the phases their children go through. Knowing what to expect from their children will equip parents to meet the challenges presented by the natural maturation process.

Learning is not a simple process, but a natural one. It is amazing how children spontaneously move through the process. Knowing the intellectual stages God designed can help parents provide varied learning opportunities through their daily routine. Knowing what to expect also gives parents the opportunity (or an edge) to prepare themselves and their environment for the next stage.

LET'S REVIEW

1. Intellectually, what is an infant like at birth? At 6 months, 12 months, 2 or 3 years?

2. What is the relationship between the baby's perception (learning through the senses) and actual experiences?

3. Why is curiosity so vital to a toddler's mental growth?

4. Why does a toddler interpret his experiences from a self-centered point of view?

5. What is the role of memory in learning?

Study 6

Learning From Children

What does it take to catch the interest of a young child? Not much, really. A bright color, a pretty flower, or a pleasant voice usually capture the attention of a small child. Even bugs and rocks may do the job! A toddler can spend a good bit of time with a simple activity, like filling and refilling a bucket with sand. He may bring you what seems to be an ordinary pebble for examination, and will be very disappointed if you don't share his enthusiasm.

Sometimes parents have been guilty of wanting to rush their children into growing up. They feel that maturity is the answer to everything. But is it? There is something to be said for qualities possessed by children, such as childlike faith, acceptance, and trust. Many positive attributes can be learned from children. Parenthood provides a golden opportunity to observe and learn from children as they grow and develop.

A RENEWED FAITH

Children accept things at face value. If parents teach them God created the heavens and the earth, they don't question it. They are taught Jesus died to save us and they believe it. When presented with God's rules to live by, they accept them.

1. Luke 18:16,17 discusses the importance of having a childlike response to God. What is the difference between being childlike and being immature?

2. Why is it important to have a childlike faith?

Children are happy to give God credit for all He has done. When children have been taught to give praise and worship to God, most eagerly do. Watching a child's enthusiastic response to God in Sunday School and church should be a motivation for adults.

3. According to Psalm 8:2, why do children respond in praise so freely?

4. Second Samuel 6:1-23 describes a grown man worshiping in an exuberant "childlike manner." Read this passage and answer the following questions:

What caused David to act as he did?

What was the reaction of his wife?

How did David respond to criticism of his worship style?

5. What are some things that hinder you regarding freedom in worship?

Young children have a willingness to believe. They have a natural tendency to have confidence in their parents and to adopt their ideas and values. Skepticism is only developed after individuals have witnessed inconsistencies in the ones they trusted.

6. Many adults are skeptical because of the failures of others. Read Hebrews 6:13-20. What confidence does this passage give concerning the faithfulness of God?

Parents can learn from the childlike faith evident in their children. The faith of children is simple and uncluttered–they simply believe. Children express no doubt and readily accept Christ and His Word. God never fails. He is always working things together for our good. As children put trust in their parents, so should parents put trust in their Heavenly Father.

Sometimes parents discourage a child's faith. They are afraid he doesn't understand what he is doing, or he is too young to comprehend a commitment to Christ. Instead of demoralizing the child's faith, parents need to provide guidance, support, and encouragement. Also, parents need to realize that through the Holy Spirit, God deals wisely with the heart of a child.

7. Read Matthew 18:6. In what ways might a parent hinder the spiritual development of a child?

Children love their parents unconditionally. Even children who are raised in deplorable and abusive circumstances usually have genuine love for their parents.

God's love is also unconditional. His acceptance of us is not dependent on our being able to do, say, or be the "right" thing. God loves us, and is willing to accept us just as we are.

It is imperative that parents love and accept their children regardless of imperfections, problems, disappointments, or difficult situations. Full acceptance because of unconditional love is a quality which can be strengthened by observing young children.

8. According to Luke 9:47,48, how does one's treatment of children reflect one's relationship with God?

A REFRESHED ATTITUDE

Children can also teach their parents in the area of attitudes. Small children tend to be genuinely humble. They haven't yet picked up the "airs" sometimes seen in older children and adults.

Young children are comfortable being themselves with all their positive and negative traits. Transparency is a trait encouraged in the Scriptures (Philippians 3:1-11). God accepts us as we are–nothing more, nothing less. A person with genuine humility recognizes he is not worthy of God's attention, but accepts God's grace as a gift. He recognizes that God is the source of all he has and all he is.

Children are candid with their problems and boldly approach their parents asking for solutions to those problems. Children are equally as bold with their displays of love and affection. Parents need to recognize their need of help and adopt a similar boldness toward their Heavenly Father.

9. According to Matthew 18:1-4, on what basis does God determine an individual's greatness?

Another lesson many adults could relearn from their children is forgiveness. Toddlers and young preschoolers are very forgiving. They may be upset over some real or perceived injustice, but they get over it quickly. The hurt is pardoned and forgotten.

Unfortunately, as the child "matures," grudges may be harbored. This is particularly true in dealing with his peers. The older preschooler may attempt revenge against the offender.

A combination of factors cause this development. Improved memory makes it easier to recall the incident. Improvement in complex thinking gives the child the ability to plot retribution. The child's egocentric nature makes it easy to view the situation with a self-serving sense of fairness. This is one example of behavior common to the fallen nature of man–lost and without Christ. Even a child is subject to the "old nature."

As parents we must practice forgiveness. Occasionally our children will cause us pain and disappointment. We must forgive them and provide another opportunity to make better choices.

10. Why is forgiveness so difficult?

Children and adults alike need the power of Christ to make them new creatures. As Christ forgave us, we too can be forgiving and compassionate to others.

11. Read Ephesians 4:31,32. What is God's solution to anger, bitterness, and slander?

12. Why is forgiveness of others fundamental in the Christian's growth? How can we help our children in this area?

A RESTORED APPRECIATION

In the beginning of time, God demonstrated His love through creation. He established an environment which would supply the physical needs of His people. The things God created were wonderful, admirable, and good. It was a big "playground" for His creation to explore!

The first family was given the responsibility to care for the land. Their respect for God and His creation was demonstrated by their concern for the Garden. After a period of time, however, the splendor of the Garden was dimmed by Adam and Eve's fixation on obtaining more than they already had. Unfortunately, this is a path followed by many as they walk the path from childhood to becoming an adult. Children can help parents recapture their appreciation of creation and respect for that which God has provided.

A toddler's curiosity propels him into exploring God's world. He wants to find out about the grass, the rocks, the cats, and dogs. A young child's favorite excursion may be to a farm or zoo where he can see a wide variety of God's creations. The preschooler asks "why" and "how" things are the way they are. The child thrives on discovering God's world. As the child learns to appreciate creation, he develops a respect for created things. Most importantly the child gains a respect for the Creator.

13. Read Genesis 1:21-31. What attitude does God model concerning His creation?

Adults who view nature through the eyes of children may renew sensitivity and appreciation for the wonders of nature. Taking time to catch snowflakes, build snowmen, play with puppies, examine blades of grass, and count the colors of autumn leaves will refocus our perspective of what God has provided.

14. As you reflect back on your childhood, what aspects of God's creation most fascinated you?

As we experience God's creation, we will develop a stronger appreciation for His creative genius. Our respect for creation is based on our respect of the Creator. With this respect comes proper use and care of His creation. He expects us to avoid misuse or abuse.

15. What do you think it means to "respect God's creation" in practical terms?

SUMMARY

Some adults think parenting is a one-way street. They feel the grown-ups are the only ones to give, with the children merely being receivers. This is far from the truth. Parents have the primary teaching responsibility; however, they are also to be learners!

Lessons in appreciation, humility, and curiosity can be invaluable. As parents look at the world through the eyes of a child, they are reminded of the simple but precious things of life.

Parents need to make the most of each day by receiving the most from each moment. They should be open-minded and receptive to the things God may show them through their children. Determine to look at the world through the eyes of your children, to see and hear with a fresh perspective.

The beauty of this perspective is learning from our parenting experiences. We model desirable, Christlike characteristics to our children. Who but our Lord Jesus Christ could have designed such an arrangement?

LET'S REVIEW

1. What traits in young children help adults better appreciate God's creation?

2. What is the role of childlike faith in approaching God?

3. As children grow up, what distracts them from the simple, faith-building elements of childhood?

4. What is humility?

5. How can we teach our children to forgive?

STUDY 7

DEVELOPING COMMUNICATION PATTERNS

A mother and her 4-year-old son headed home after a long day. "Mommy, Jimmy's dog has new puppies! He said I could have one! Can I, Mommy? Please, can I? I'll take good care of it!"

"Um. That's nice," Mom responded.

"Can I, Mommy? Please!"

"I–uh, do what, Son? Can you what?"

"The puppy, Mommy. Can I?"

"Puppy? What puppy?"

Compare this conversation to another one between the same mother and son, several years later. Mom has just picked her son up from school.

"Hi, Son! How was school?"

"Hm? Oh...OK."

"We are going to have your favorite meal tonight."

"Hm? That's great. Oh, yeah. Ah, Mom, Jim asked me to come over and shoot some hoops. We'll just grab a burger or something."

"You didn't hear a word I said, did you? You never do."

COMMUNICATION TAKES PRACTICE

The previous dramatization illustrates the communication which develops in all too many families. This situation can be avoided with awareness and planning.

Communication is of critical importance in any relationship, whether between husband and wife, parent and child, employee and employer, or God and man. The quality of any relationship is largely determined by the level of communication. The primary way to develop communication skills is to practice.

The best time to begin cultivating quality communication is the day your baby is born. Talk to your child from the very beginning. The interaction and the foundation being built are extremely important, even if your child doesn't understand everything.

There is some indication that we should talk to babies before birth! Research has shown that babies who are talked to prenatally are more sensitive to the human voice, especially a woman's.

The enjoyment and success of communication will depend on several factors. One is your tone of voice. It conveys mood and emotion to your baby. Another important aspect of your communication is touch. Physical touch, such as cuddling and caressing, is a nurturing aspect of your conversation.

Eye contact is another important aspect. Newborns especially love to study your face and eyes. This provides an opportunity to get to know you. The child will eventually learn to associate your expressions with your varied moods.

Initially, the baby will respond more to tone of voice and touch than to what you say. Even as his understanding increases, he will still interpret what you really mean by your tone of voice and body language.

1. According to Deuteronomy 6:6,7, what role does communication play in a child's spiritual development?

____

____

____

2. Read Genesis 3:6-9. What caused broken communication between God and His creation?

____

____

3. How can you prevent a similar break in communication between yourself and your child?

____

____

Prior to actually talking, the baby communicates by other means. He learns how to get the attention of adults and acquire their assistance. The child becomes quite adept at getting his message across with gestures and grunts.

As the baby gets older, he will progress from producing accidental sounds to sounds which are intentional. A baby begins to communicate well before he is able to form meaningful sentences. A baby of 6 or 7 months will interact with individuals by mimicking what others do. He will engage in a pleasant communication game taking turns "talking" or making sounds.

By 7 or 8 months a baby will respond to the sound of his name and will recognize several words. Generally, the words he knows are ones he has heard repeatedly.

Between 8 and 15 months the child will say his first meaningful word. It can sometimes be hard to pinpoint the first word, as the baby makes so many sounds that resemble words.

Many 1-year-old children have a vocabulary of several words and understand many more. Some children don't begin talking until 2½x or 3 years of age. Some parents become disturbed if their child doesn't talk at an early age. If the child demonstrates increased understanding by following simple directions and requests, parents should not be concerned.

The greatest understanding will occur when parents converse on the child's level. This means using vocabulary and sentence length appropriate for the child's developmental stage. Sometimes adults tend to use long sentences that lose the child's attention. At other times, they simply say too much, overwhelming the toddler or preschooler.

4. Read 1 Corinthians 3:2. How can this Scripture be applied to developing communication with our children?

____

____

Likewise, parents can become too simplistic in their communication. The child will learn to recognize and pronounce words he has heard pronounced by those around him. If people engage in baby talk, the child's learning of the correct pronunciation will be hindered. Although baby talk seems cute to some adults, it should be used sparingly.

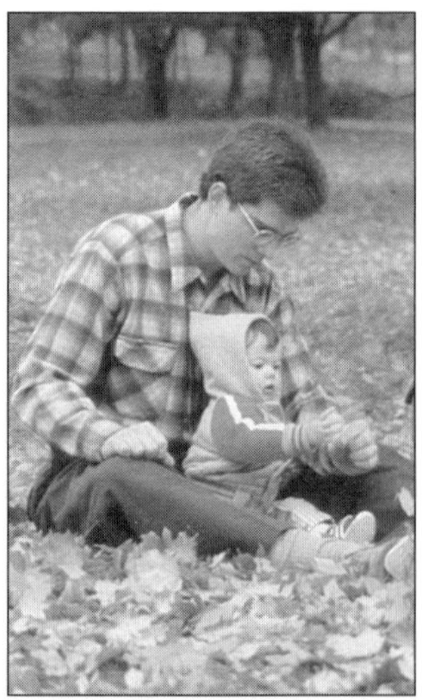

To enhance your child's language and concept development, talk about anything and everything in his world. Use words which describe color, shape, size, and texture. When you take your child to buy groceries, talk about the bright yellow lemons, the pungent onions, and the cold frozen vegetables. Make ordinary, routine excursions interesting, enjoyable learning experiences by developing creative conversation. Planned, formal lessons are not necessary. Simply take advantage of daily communication between you and your child.

Several things are achieved by this approach to communication. You help your child grasp basic intellectual concepts. He will learn about his environment. You'll find yourself having fun as you enjoy time with your child.

An additional benefit of interacting with your child is the open line of communication you are establishing. Fun, relaxed conversation today will make more serious topics easier to approach tomorrow.

COMMUNICATION: MORE THAN WORDS

Many of us are good at talking. We desire to express ourselves, our feelings, and our ideas; yet, there is much more to communication than giving words and ideas. There is also receiving words and ideas. Communication can be compared to a two-way street. Traffic needs to flow freely in both directions!

An important skill in communication is listening. Listening takes time, effort, and concentration. Effective listening must be done with the ears, the heart, and with sensitivity to the meaning conveyed by the speaker.

Listening with the heart means hearing what the other person–the child in this case–is feeling as well as what he is saying. Sensitive listening sends important messages to children. It tells them we care enough to give them our time, our attention, and our respect. It reassures them that we are deeply concerned about what they feel and think.

True listening involves some risks. It means that at times we might hear some things we don't want to hear such as, "I'm mad at you, Daddy!" or, "Mommy, you hurt my feelings!" Often we would rather avoid dealing with these issues, but once they are communicated, we must resolve them.

5. James 1:19 offers excellent advice regarding effective communication skills. Record the three-pronged advice below.

____

____

6. How would application of the advice recorded in James 1:19 develop respect and trust between a parent and child?

____

____

____

Sincere listening helps remove the masks we are inclined to hide behind. It may open conversation that encourages us to be genuine with each other. Real communication encourages honesty and openness.

Lines of communication must be kept open and orderly. There will be occasional misunderstandings. Things may be said that should have been left unsaid. Whenever this type of problem threatens communication between you and your child, take immediate action. It is imperative to your relationship that hurts be mended and communication lines are kept open.

7. According to Matthew 5:23,24 and Matthew 6:14,15, who is responsible to mend broken relationships?

____

____

____

Basically, keeping the lines open means listening and giving attention to your child. This does not mean allowing the child to be rude or to interrupt conversations of others. However, it does mean being sensitive to and tuned in to your child's needs. Often a child's conversation may seem trite, even insignificant. However, from his point of view his concerns are very important.

Parents should attempt to develop the ability to look at the child's world through his eyes. When this is accomplished, it becomes easier to understand why the child is captivated with seemingly small and simple things. Because of the child's limited experiences and maturity, things adults may view as trivial may be monumental to him.

It is important that parents cultivate a child's communication development through attentive listening.

THE RESULTS OF COMMUNICATION

Communication, like other interpersonal skills, can be used wisely or unwisely. These skills can have positive or negative effects. The patterns of communication with our children can either build them up or tear them down. Because communication is a powerful tool, we need to be cautious in its use and application.

Children are sensitive and are affected by the things we tell them. The self-esteem of a child will suffer when he is subjected to put-downs and belittling comments. Parents exercise the most influence in the life of a young child. Their words have a powerful effect on the development of the child's self-concept. Parents must avoid careless speech and actions.

8. James 3:9,10 clearly states the tongue can easily be used for evil or for good. What precautions can parents take to avoid hurting their children?

____

____

____

Directing positive comments toward the child is important. When reprimand is necessary, focus on the inappropriate deed rather than the personhood of the child. Replace phrases such as, "You are such a bad boy for doing that!" with "What you did was wrong!" This separates the action from the child himself. If he becomes convinced he is a "bad boy," his behavior will reflect his belief. If he realizes his choice was wrong, he can try to make better choices in the future.

A word of caution! As Christians, we are to avoid distorted humanistic teachings about the worth and goodness of human beings. Mankind is not inherently good. This was proven when the very first humans chose to do evil. Fortunately, God in His grace sent His Son to bear the consequences of the poor choices of those who willingly repent and follow Him.

It is important to teach children that they are responsible for the poor choices they make. Children should be taught that they can ask God to forgive them for their sin. This takes care of the spiritual consequences of sin. Children should also be taught that in addition to spiritual consequences, there are physical and social consequences for wrong choices. Ideally, our actions should mirror our relationship with Christ.

9. **Genesis 3 records the first occurrence of sin. Genesis 3:21 indicates that Adam and Eve were forgiven "spiritually." What was the "physical" consequence for their sin recorded in Genesis 3:23?**

____

____

Communication provides opportunities to share personal values and beliefs. As parents, we are to establish openness between us and our children enabling us to teach them the things we cherish. It is not enough to simply tell our children what they should believe. We must be willing to present biblical evidence to support our values and beliefs. It is only fair to the child to support our beliefs with reasons they can, or will in time, be able to comprehend.

If communication between parent and child has been positive, it is likely that children will adopt their parent's positions. Don't be surprised if even the youngest child asks seemingly impossible questions. Be open and honest. Never revert to "because I said so!" answers. If you are unable to answer some question, take the time to discover the answer together. Never underestimate the power of the Holy Spirit. He is more than capable of enlightening the mind and spirit of even the youngest child.

10. **Read Deuteronomy 5:1. Moses provides a fail-proof formula for righteous living. What three steps are given in Moses' command to the Israelites?**

____

____

____

11. **How could the formula outlined in Deuteronomy 5:1 be helpful in the life of a family?**

____

____

SUMMARY

The early years of the child's life is the time to develop communication patterns for the future. Parents' goals should include establishing open lines of communication and building a framework of sensitivity, openness, respect, and trust.

Parents can teach much through what they say to their children. By discussing what is going on around him, the child learns concepts and language. Also, the parent-child bond is enhanced, creating healthy social and emotional development.

Listening is an important part of communication. Responding to his queries aids the child's growth and development of spiritual values.

As parents, let us realize the power of communication. May we seek God for guidance in developing healthy, lifelong, communication patterns.

LET'S REVIEW

1. Why is communication with our children so vital?

2. What ways can parents communicate with a 6-month-old? a 3-year-old?

3. What is the parent's role in listening?

4. How does open communication aid in the teaching of values and beliefs to our children?

STUDY 8

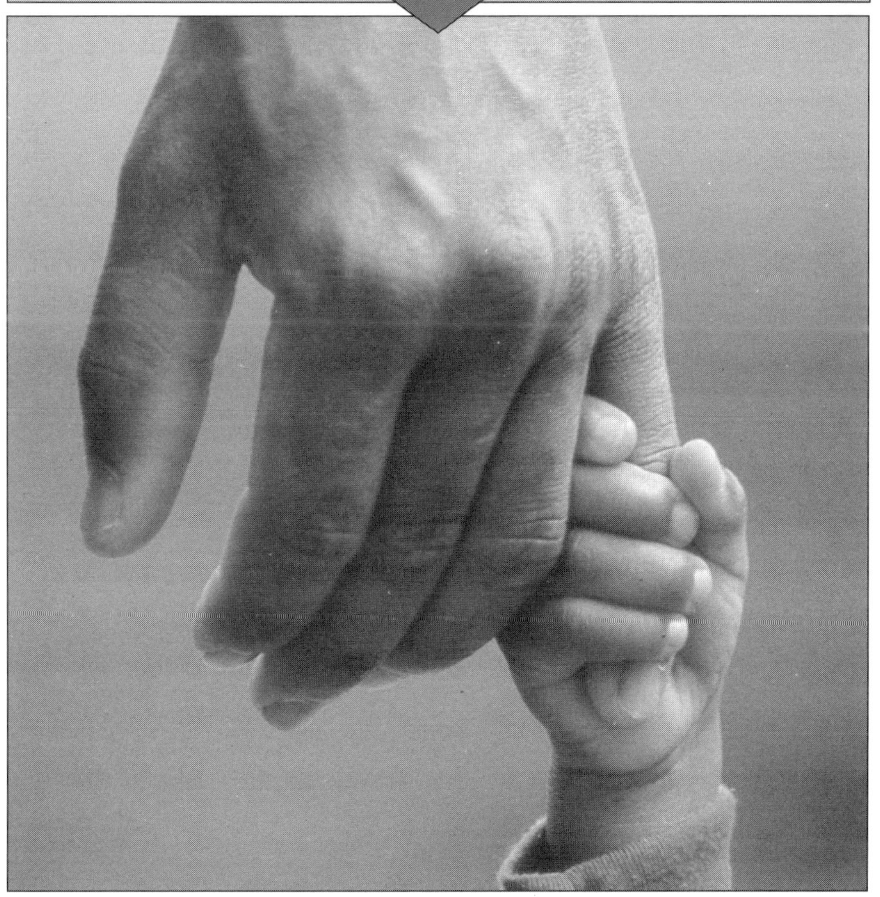

GUIDANCE AND DISCIPLINE

One of the most challenging areas of parenting is providing appropriate guidance and discipline. Advice on the subject ranges from extremely conservative to the outermost limits of liberal thinking. "Experts" have a way of making their suggested philosophies and methodologies sound reasonable and convincing. This can make it very difficult for new parents (and some not-so-new!) to sort out good advice and to come to terms with this area of responsibility.

THE IMPORTANCE OF DISCIPLINE

Providing proper guidance and discipline is not optional–it is essential. Some parents try to avoid facing the needs their children have in the area of discipline. Perhaps these parents unrealistically fear rejection or resentment by their children. Whatever the motivation, the results are always disastrous. Children need and actually desire to know what behaviors are expected, even though they may sometimes choose to do otherwise.

1. According to Proverbs 1:8,9 and 3:1,2, what benefits await children who respond positively to parental guidance?

___

___

___

Why is so much incongruity seen in various approaches to discipline? Perhaps it is because discipline touches on the very essence of human nature. After all it was a lack of self-discipline that caused Adam and Eve to sin in the first place!

2. According to 1 Samuel 15:22,23, why is discipline so crucial in an individual's overall growth and development?

___

___

Children aren't born with self-discipline skills. They do not instinctively know how to behave. They have no concept of right and wrong. It is a parent's God-given responsibility to provide continuous instruction in these areas. Only when they have done their part can they expect to see their children blossom into productive citizens and members of God's family of believers. Providing guidance is an ongoing aspect of parenting.

Building a solid foundation and framework of communication, sensitivity, and mutual respect in the child's early years can help him develop and mature in the future.

3. Read Proverbs 23:13,14 and write this passage in your own words.

___

___

DISCIPLINE TECHNIQUES

Several techniques have been found helpful in the area of discipline and guidance. In time, these practices can become a comfortable part of your parenting style. Two key elements of effective discipline are encouraging good behavior and setting reasonable limits.

Encouraging Good Behavior

Active steps can be taken to encourage desired behavior. A very important step is to be a good example. Children learn many things–including some we don't intend for them to learn–by observing the people closest to them. Parents should practice traits they wish their children to develop. Children are great imitators. If their parents are honest, sensitive, thoughtful, mannerly, truthful, industrious, eat their vegetables, read their Bibles, and pray, the children are likely to adopt similar values and habits. There needs to be congruency between what parents say and what they do. Exemplifying these traits speaks louder than words in demonstrating to their children what is really important.

Another way to encourage good behavior is to make sure the child understands what is expected. Keep in mind his vocabulary level. Also, explanations should be short, simple, and age-appropriate. A small child can't focus on or mentally process too much at a time. It is helpful to ask simple questions for clarification. Feedback from the child will help you see if he understands.

Parents often have greater success if they focus on what they want the child to do rather than what not to do. For example, a 3-year-old may often seem to forget the rule, "Don't run in the house!" He may do better with, "Walk in the house." The reason involves the verbs, or action words. A small child is very busy, always on the move. Action words like "run" readily catch his attention when words such as "don't" fail to make much of an impression. The message that is planted in the toddler's and preschooler's minds may be exactly the opposite of what the parents really wanted!

4. Compare Deuteronomy 5:7-21 with Mark 12:29-31. Each passage communicates the same truth. Which set of commands would be easier to follow? Why?

____

____

Positive reinforcement is another tool to use in encouraging good behavior. A smile, a hug, or a pat on the back all send the message to your child that you are happy with his behavior. A small child really desires to please his parents. When he recognizes a particular behavior made his parents happy, he will be more likely to repeat it.

Positive reinforcement does not mean bribery. Some parents make a habit of promising a treat or toy if the child is good. This method teaches the child to behave because of a tangible reward, rather than simply because it is the right thing to do. Also, he learns how to manipulate adults who use bribery by "bargaining" for what he wants. The child learns some lessons here, but not the ones intended!

It is fine to occasionally surprise your child with a special treat. A reward showing appreciation for exemplary behavior is different from a bribe. An occasional, unexpected act of recognition lets your child know that his efforts are appreciated.

Giving your child the opportunity to make some decisions also promotes good behavior. Making simple choices, such as which shirt to wear, or what fruit to eat, gives the child a feeling of power. He sees that he too has some control over his world. This is important as the toddler becomes more independent. He needs opportunities to learn how to wisely use his abilities. He also needs practice for making more difficult choices at a later time.

Initially, offer the child a choice between two selections. Make sure that whichever he chooses is acceptable to you. Asking, "What do you want for lunch?"

is too open ended. The child may select something you don't have or that would take too long to prepare. Limiting the available choices to ones you can provide keeps you from having to go back on your word–or spending hours preparing lunch!

Setting Limits

The second technique of discipline and guidance involves setting limits. The simple truth is, children need limits. Limits provide boundaries to help them–and us–measure personal actions to determine if the behavior is acceptable or not.

When setting limits, consider the child's age and developmental stage. Obviously, more freedoms can be extended to the child as he gets older and displays more responsible behavior. A toddler, for example, requires constant adult supervision. A 4-year-old, however, can usually play alone for short periods of time.

No matter how good a job parents do, children will occasionally misbehave. The way these situations are handled determines the type and frequency of future occurrences.

Handling misbehavior also affects our children in less direct ways. They learn interpersonal skills from our example. They see how to cope with conflict and how to approach people when there is disagreement. Their self-esteem is also affected by the methods used in dealing with their misconduct. It is important that parents realize the far-reaching effects of discipline.

5. The apostle Paul wrote a letter to the Corinthian church reprimanding them for ungodly acts. Read 2 Corinthians 7:8-12 and summarize the results of this act of discipline.

____

____

6. Describe how discipline has helped shape your life.

____

____

____

Dealing With Misbehavior

Distraction works well with children too young to understand why some things are off-limits. When toddlers are fascinated with knobs on the stereo or with Aunt Jane's string of pearls, divert their attention with a favorite toy or activity. Concealing the off-limit item or removing the children bodily from the forbidden activity to something appropriate can be very effective for babies and toddlers under 18 months.

Sometimes natural consequences are sufficient. If your child has been taught not to pet strange dogs, but he runs up to one and is nipped, the painful experience is enough of a punishment. He found out–the hard way–your instructions were for his benefit.

Some behaviors are best ignored. If the purpose of the behavior is to get attention, and it doesn't work, the child will try other approaches. When he uses a

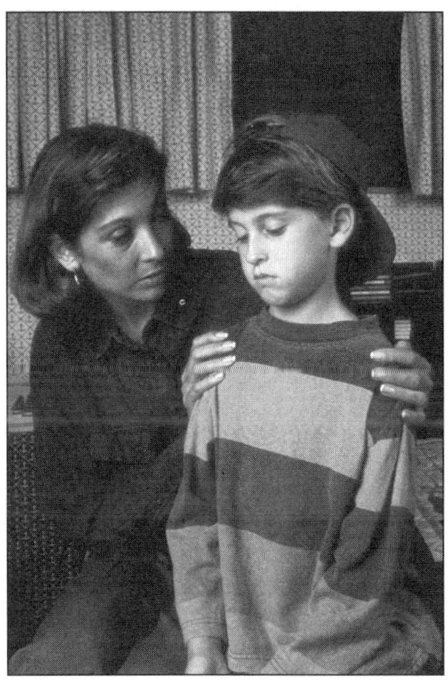

means of which you approve, be sure to give positive attention to help reinforce the desired behavior.

Of course, behaviors that won't cause injury or damage can be ignored. Examples include temper tantrums and whining. It can be hard to ignore an annoying behavior because many of us weren't raised this way. However, this method can get excellent results.

A method that works better with older toddlers and preschoolers is "time out." This technique provides children the opportunity to think about the offense and the consequence as well as the chance to calm down if upset. Many parents use one particular location as the "time-out seat." Being removed from an enjoyable activity is often enough to make children think twice before committing the infraction again. Keep the amount of "time out" reasonable; generally, 1 minute per year of age is suitable. More than that may result in frustration, causing children to lose sight of the original issue.

A method especially appropriate for misbehavior involving the misuse or abuse of objects or freedoms is loss of privilege. For example, if the child hits people with his toy hammer, put the hammer away until tomorrow. Or, if a 4-year-old leaves the yard where he was supposed to stay, he should lose the privilege of playing outside for the rest of the day. This close correlation between the offense and the consequence is especially effective. Be sure to verbally explain why the action was taken.

7. What does the writer of Proverbs say about physical discipline regarding its usage and purpose? (Proverbs 13:24; 22:15; 23:13,14; 29:15)

____

____

8. How do you feel about spankings? When are they appropriate? What actions would generate usage of this type of discipline?

____

____

Many questions have been raised about the wisdom of spanking and other forms of physical discipline. Not too long ago, the validity of spanking was not in doubt. Today, however, society looks at the issue differently.

Certainly, spanking can cause problems. Many feel that it shows children it is acceptable for a bigger person to hit a smaller one. Unfortunately, spanking for some parents becomes abusive. Another problem can be overuse and overdependency. Adults who find themselves swatting their children constantly, or using intimidation tactics, are not disciplining them, but doing them harm.

Others believe that the use of spanking is indicated in Scripture. Those who use spanking effectively see it as one part in their overall approach to discipline. When used with wisdom and sensitivity, it can prevent undesirable behavior.

Parents will have to examine the issue for themselves. No matter which choice is made, some won't agree. Be prepared for some criticism.

Parents who decide to utilize spanking need to keep several things in mind. First of all, when spanking, remain calm and self-controlled. The child needs to clearly see the action as a consequence of his misbehavior, not as a result of the parent's anger. The spanking should be administered on the buttocks only; swats to any other location are totally unacceptable. There should never be any marks left (welts, bruises, etc.). Lastly, spankings should be reserved for very serious offenses. They should not be used as a daily part of discipline.

Parents who decide not to spank need to have a definite plan of action when tested by their children. Adults who were spanked as children may resort to physical punishment when confronted with a difficult situation. Parents tend to parent as they were parented. If changes are desired, a clear plan needs to be in mind. The other methods described, time out, distraction, etc., can be very effective.

9. Read Hebrews 12:4-13. Summarize the writer of Hebrews' comparison of God's discipline and that of a parent.

____

____

DISCIPLINING ONESELF

God never makes mistakes. The discipline He uses is always timely and appropriate.

Unfortunately, the same thing can't be said for human parents. At times, each of us will err. We might react too quickly before getting all the facts, or we may respond too harshly. Mistakes happen. Then what?

It takes a confident person to say, "I'm sorry. I made a mistake." Handling mistakes correctly provides an opportunity to continue teaching children Christian character. When children hear parents ask for forgiveness and apologize for human frailties, they learn how to cope with their own shortcomings. Praying together afterwards models Christian character.

Parents have always desired to ensure their children's successful growth and development. Job is a good Old Testament example of a father who provided his children with guidance and direction.

10. Job demonstrated his concern for his children through actions recorded in Job 1:4,5. What are some practical ways parents can assist their children spiritually today?

____

____

____

____

Parents should be aware of certain methods of discipline and guidance that are essential to their child's growth.

One important element is consistency. Consistency requires handling situations in the same manner each time they occur. If a child is reprimanded for a behavior one day, the same behavior shouldn't be ignored or rewarded the next. Though not always easy, it is necessary to be as uniform as possible. This helps the child learn what is actually expected, and that it is in his best interest to adhere to the rules. When the child learns the consequences will always be the same, he is less likely to test the limits. Being consistent helps the child develop trust in his parents. He knows they mean what they say and can depend on it.

Another valuable element of successful discipline is unity. Parents should settle their differences regarding limits and discipline privately. The children should see a single mind in Mom and Dad, otherwise, children are quick to learn how to manipulate their parents. They will soon figure out how to use one parent against the other to get what they want. Parents in support of one another is reassuring to their children.

11. Read Matthew 19:5. What principle is taught in this passage and how should this principle affect selection of discipline procedures?

____

____

____

____

____

____

The last element to consider is prayer, a necessity of Christian living. It is imperative in parenting. Prayer is a key to building a foundation of respect and trust in the parent-child relationship. Prayer is essential in communing with God, who gives us strength, guidance, and wisdom. Taking time to pray in every circumstance allows God to work in us and through us as we meet the challenges of discipline.

When our children see us pray, both on a regular basis and in specific situations, they learn to lean on God. They discover that God is able to help them with everything, even their behavior.

SUMMARY

Providing guidance and discipline is essential in raising children. God gives us help in getting the job done. Parental guidance includes being a good example, setting reasonable limits, and using proper techniques when dealing with misbehavior. Parents are more successful if they are consistent, if they present a united front, and if prayer is an integral part of their lives.

Parenting can seem like an impossible task. It can even evoke fear at times. Be assured that you can be a good parent. God will provide the strength and wisdom as you consistently rely on Him.

LET'S REVIEW

1. When do guidance and discipline begin?

2. How can desired behavior be encouraged?

3. Which techniques for handling misbehavior do you think would be most effective? Why?

4. Why is consistency so important?

5. Why is parental unity critical in achieving success?

6. Why is prayer essential in successful parenting?

STUDY 9

TEACHING OUR CHILDREN ABOUT JESUS

Love for children is a great motivator. Most parents desire to provide attractive clothing, wholesome food, and a comfortable home for their children. Most also want to supply additional nonessentials to enrich their children's lives. Parents not only consider these things their responsibility but take delight in doing them.

One obligation parents have causes all others to pale in comparison. This is the responsibility and privilege of introducing their children to Christ. As important as it is to meet physical, emotional, and intellectual needs, helping children meet spiritual needs through Christ as Savior has eternal significance. Like other aspects of parenting, skills can be developed that will help this become a comfortable, natural responsibility. More importantly, the Holy Spirit will provide guidance and direction to those who ask.

PARENTS LEADING CHILDREN BY EXAMPLE

A common thread running throughout these studies has been "example." Children learn much by observing and following patterns modeled by their parents. They find out about many subjects, ranging from kindness, to good hygiene, to Christianity.

To be effective, parents' Christianity must be genuine. It is important for children to see their parents practicing their Christian faith in every aspect of daily life. Being keen observers, children notice if their parents' lives don't measure up to what they claim to believe.

This doesn't mean parents must be perfect; after all, the foundation of Christianity is Christ's forgiveness of sin. No one is capable of perfection. However, there should be consistency between what a person says and what he does.

Daily, we have opportunities to teach our children about the things of God. They learn from seeing how we spend our time, from observing our priorities, and from hearing our topics of conversation. To be effective, parents must conduct their business and personal lives in a Christlike manner.

We can take advantage of daily routine to teach our children about God. During a normal day, there are many opportunities to express appreciation to God for His many blessings and to give credit to God for what He has done. Expressing thanks for the beauty of a rose, the warmth of the sunshine, or for the family we enjoy, shows our children that we recognize the One who is responsible.

The time to teach children about the characteristics of God is when they are young. They need to know that their Heavenly Father is a loving, caring God who is concerned about every area of their lives.

Helping our children see our standards and values are based on biblical principles gives them a firm foundation to develop their own moral codes.

1. Read Deuteronomy 6:4-9. How can you put these instructions into practice in your family?

____

____

____

Wise parents should not overlook church attendance. Going to church and Sunday School sends several messages. Our children see we are willing and eager to give time to worship and training. This is another opportunity to teach by example that God is a priority in our lives.

Training through the church reinforces concepts taught at home. Receiving information from multiple sources intensifies the impact. Children should learn to respect other adults who believe in God and His Word.

The church nursery can be a great asset to your own personal growth. After determining the safety of the nursery and the reliability of the staff, feel free to place your child in their loving care. Although your child may resist at first, soon he will feel at home in that setting. Having your small child in the nursery allows you to focus on the Sunday School lesson or pastor's sermon without distraction. An excellent way to reinforce the value of the nursery is for you to volunteer your services there.

As your toddler outgrows the church nursery, he will be ready for his own Sunday School class. Here he will learn about God through Bible stories and songs.

Sunday School provides reinforcement and enrichment for what your child has been taught at home. Sunday School provides a setting for socialization which is an important part of your child's development. There your child will not only learn Christian concepts but will have an opportunity to put those concepts into practice.

Children's Church is another valuable tool in the spiritual development of a child. In Children's Church, a child is given age-appropriate activities designed for spiritual growth. Creative methods are used to present Christian teachings. Children's Church provides a forum to learn about worship and praise and an opportunity to experiment in a safe environment.

2. How can parents help prepare their child for participation in the nursery, Sunday School, and Children's Church?

____

____

____

PARENTS LEADING CHILDREN IN SPIRITUAL DEVOTION

One of the most important ways to influence our children for Christ is earnest prayer. Prayer should be a regular, natural part of our lives and its power should never be underestimated. Our children need to see us pray at mealtime, bedtime, for specific needs, and with thanksgiving, both at church and at home. It is a powerful example when our children see us put our faith and trust in God. The image of us praying will make a lasting impression on our children.

It should be natural for Christian parents to pray for their children. An awareness of the difficulties and risks in growing up should keep parents on their knees! Parents should also pray with their children, modeling for them how to pray, and giving them opportunity to approach God. Encouraging the development of a personal prayer life while children are young increases the chances they will become praying adults, ready to face later challenges.

The value of learning Scripture is immeasurable. When Scripture verses are memorized, they are available for recall in time of distress or difficulty. The Scriptures offer comfort, encouragement, and guidance.

3. According to Deuteronomy 31:12,13 and Psalm 78:5-7, why is it vital to communicate spiritual truths to our children?

____

____

There are several tools available to help teach Scripture to children. One especially effective method is through Scripture songs. Children love music and will readily learn simple verses through this medium.

Preschool children can begin memorizing short, simple Scriptures. Make the task pleasurable like it is a game, not a chore. Avoid putting too much pressure or unreasonable demands on them. When studying and memorizing the Scriptures ceases being pleasant, learning will slow down or even stop.

 **4. According to Psalm 119:11, what is one of the benefits of memorizing Scripture?**

____

____

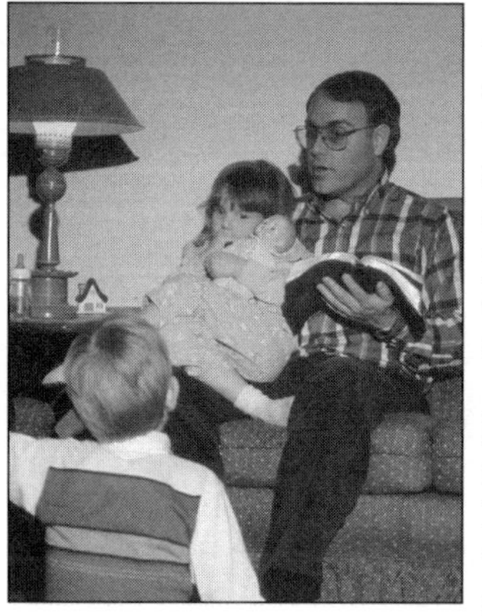

Another way to present biblical truths is through Bible stories. Even though Scripture memorization isn't usually included, children will come to know the story plots in detail. The children will see how our sovereign God has worked in the lives of people throughout history. This pleasant activity provides opportunities for parents and children to discuss what was read and for questions to be asked.

Bible story books are available for every age level. For the younger child, books should include colorful, uncluttered pictures. The wording should be simple and clear. Make reading the stories a regular part of the child's day. The dividends will be great for such an investment!

5. Read Exodus 10:1,2 and Joshua 4:1-7. Bible stories are records of God's activities in the lives of His people. Make a list of events in your life that illustrate God's faithfulness and that you can communicate to your children. Plan to add to this list as the years progress.

____

____

____

PARENTS LEADING CHILDREN TO CHRIST

Most adults wonder how to approach leading their child to Christ. They wonder not only about what to say, but how to say it. Some fear that they will say or do the "wrong" thing and pull their child away from God. Others are fearful of pushing the child into a decision "too early."

Our child will cue us as to his readiness. One good indicator is his questions. Whenever and whatever the child asks, we need to be willing to answer. Keeping our answers simple and age-appropriate will enhance the child's comprehension. Follow the child's lead by adding more information as needed. When the child seems satisfied with the information given, and has no more to ask at this time, let the issue rest. After he has digested what he heard, and the Holy Spirit has worked in his heart and mind, he may come back with additional questions. As long as communication is kept open, the child will feel comfortable initiating more conversation.

It is imperative that parents depend on the Lord for wisdom and guidance as they direct their child. God sees into the heart and mind of a child and can offer direction to parents which will most effectively address the child's needs.

6. Read Mark 10:13-16. Summarize Jesus' attitude toward the children and their needs.

Listening is an important skill in determining your child's readiness for learning about and accepting salvation. The gospel is intentionally simple. God did not want to exclude anyone from being able to accept salvation, including your child.

Children will indicate their readiness by the questions they ask and the interest they show in the things of God. When they demonstrate an understanding that Jesus loves them and died so their sins can be forgiven, they are ready to accept Christ.

The Holy Spirit can stir the hearts of adults and children alike. If parents are sensitive to what the Lord is doing in their children, they will be available to support and encourage their spiritual growth.

Leading your child in a salvation prayer should not be difficult. Use a short, simple prayer that guides the child in asking for forgiveness and requesting that Jesus come into his life. Close with giving thanks for what God has done.

In the future, the child may desire to repeat the sinner's prayer again. Adults may wonder or even worry about this repetition. After all, wasn't the child saved? Or did he backslide? As the child matures and develops greater understanding of what salvation means, he may feel a need to pray again. It doesn't mean that the early prayer was ineffective; it just means that with greater understanding the child has a new desire to communicate his dependence and gratitude to God.

Throughout your child's spiritual development, trust the Holy Spirit to work in your child as the time is right. Trust your child to respond accordingly, while you give him guidance, love, and support.

SUMMARY

A parent's life is the most influential example a child will ever have. A parent's Christianity will be examined for consistency. Regular church and Sunday School attendance will also impact a child's spiritual development. The lessons and concepts reinforced by these services and classes can have eternal significance.

Learning to pray and developing an appreciation for Scripture should be accomplished early in a child's life. Family devotions, stories, and songs are just a few methods which may be employed to instill these valuable habits.

It is a great privilege to be an integral part of shaping a person's spiritual life. This is especially true when that person is your own child. Taking advantage of the opportunities available will result in blessings for yourself and your child.

LET'S REVIEW

1. Why is it so important for parents to provide the proper example for their children?

2. What role does the church and Sunday School play in teaching our children?

3. What are some ways we can help our children hide God's Word in their hearts?

4. What are some signs that indicate our children are ready to accept Jesus as Savior?

5. Why is prayer so important in the spiritual growth of our children?

STUDY 10

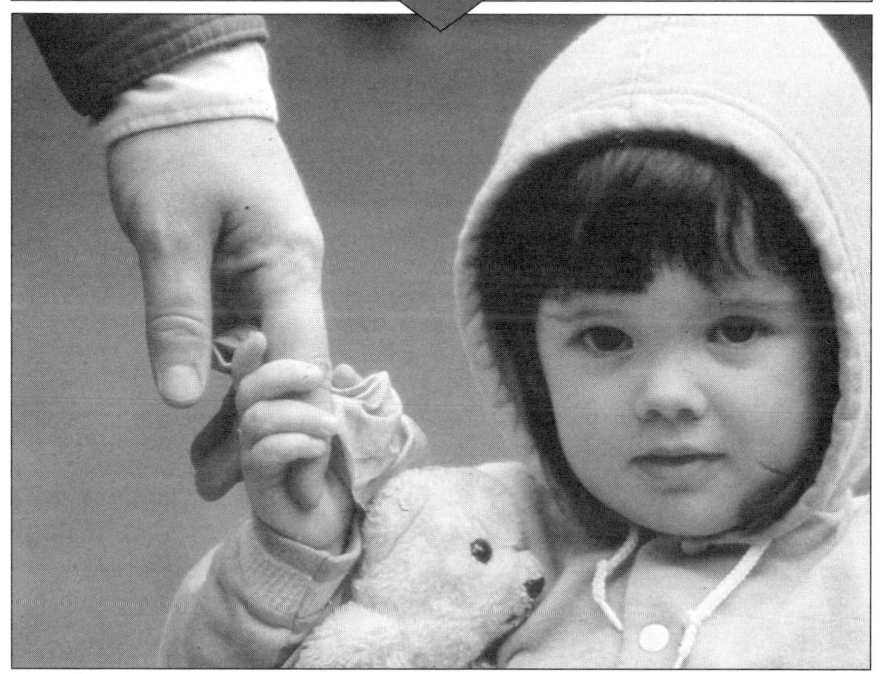

PROTECTING GOD'S GIFT

Scripture makes it clear that children are a special gift from God and are given as a blessing. God places great value on children. They should be lovingly cared for, protected, and raised in the counsel of the Lord.

Not all children are treated the way God intended. Many children are victims of adults out of control. Abuse of children is a worldwide problem. Unfortunately, this type of abuse is found in some Christian homes.

Child abuse must not be ignored. Both the abused and the abuser need help. Christian parents must be aware of the problem and seek ways to prevent further abuse.

Abuse happens for various reasons and under differing circumstances. The results, however, are always the same: children are hurt and carry scars for life. Counseling and therapy can aid recovery, but only the love and healing power of God can fully restore them to wholeness.

PREVENTING CHILD ABUSE

Prevention is always better than attempting to correct the damage. Steps can be taken by parents and caregivers to make abuse a less likely occurrence.

One way of preventing child abuse is to have a good understanding of child development. Often abuse occurs because an adult has unreasonable expectations of the child. Knowing what should be expected at different ages and stages of development helps parents deal with the frustrations often experienced in parenting.

Knowledge of children's basic needs benefits both parent and child. Parents who understand what is required in the area of physical care are less likely to neglect these needs. The same is also true of emotional, intellectual, and spiritual needs. For example, parents who understand the importance of reading to their children will probably do so. Mothers and fathers who understand the significance of human touch will hug and cuddle their children in an appropriate manner. Realizing the benefits of praying together will motivate families to do so. Parents who learn about their children's needs will experience great dividends.

1. Describe the beautiful parental illustration recorded in Isaiah 40:11. How would conformity to this parenting style prevent child abuse?

Another step which can be taken to reduce the likelihood of abuse is to plan ahead. All children will occasionally be a source of frustration and testing. Planning appropriate ways to react will reduce the chance of improper spontaneous reactions to normal childhood behavior.

2. How would a full comprehension of Jesus' teachings in Matthew 10:42 and Mark 9:37 help individuals avoid child abuse?

Child abuse is never the fault of the child. As adults, we must accept full responsibility for our actions. Adults are accountable–to family members, to legal authorities, and most certainly to God–for all that they do.

3. How would a full understanding of 2 Corinthians 5:10 help prevent child abuse?

In no area of life do we have greater accountability than in parenting. Taking responsibility for our actions, being there for our children in every respect, and seeking help from God in all circumstances are minimal expectations.

Each parent is accountable, even if his own childhood left something to be desired. There are many resources available to help people learn appropriate parenting skills. God has also promised to help those who seek to do His will.

4. What is promised to all believers in James 1:5? How does this apply to parenting?

____

____

____

TYPES OF CHILD ABUSE

Children may be victimized by several types of child abuse. Each type, though different in outward symptoms and manifestations, hurts children.

5. According to Matthew 18:1-6, what is the consequence of deliberately abusing a child?

____

____

Often, when child abuse is mentioned, physical abuse comes to mind. Beating, whipping, slapping, hitting, biting, kicking, choking, and burning all constitute physical abuse. Some of these behaviors may occur when a parent or other caregiver reaches a level of frustration resulting in loss of control. Other cases occur when an adult intentionally hurts a child.

Another form of abuse is neglect. Neglect occurs when caregivers fail to provide adequately for basic needs. The deprived needs may be physical in nature, such as lack of food, clothing, and medical care. Emotional deprivation occurs when children are not hugged, cuddled, or shown appropriate affection. All too often, neglect takes the form of disregard of children's health and safety needs. A lack of supervision, an unhealthy or unsafe environment, access to any hazardous material, or any condition that jeopardizes the child's health and safety are forms of neglect.

6. According to 1 Timothy 5:8, how is the man who neglects his family's financial needs characterized by the apostle Paul?

____

____

7. How can the principle stated in 1 Timothy 5:8 be applied to other forms of neglect on the part of parents?

____

____

Some children experience verbal abuse. This generally means saying things to children that puts them down, taunts them, or is harshly critical. This can include swearing at children, calling them derogatory names, or telling them they are dumb or stupid. Verbal abuse is often hard to detect because it leaves no physical marks. However, emotional scars may cause wounds as deep as those caused by physical abuse.

8. Ephesians 6:4 provides a specific parenting instruction. Summarize that instruction below.

____

____

Sexual abuse takes place any time an adult uses a child for his or her own sexual gratification. The actions may range from the exposing and/or fondling of private anatomy to actual intercourse.

Most cases of abuse involve parents, stepparents, other relatives, and caregivers (unfortunately, even in the church). Most abusers are not strangers; they are known to the child. It is wise for parents to be extremely cautious in selecting people to care for their child. When selecting day care or hiring a sitter, get references from reliable sources to reduce the likelihood of abuse. Those who refuse to provide references should be avoided.

CONSEQUENCES OF CHILD ABUSE

The Child

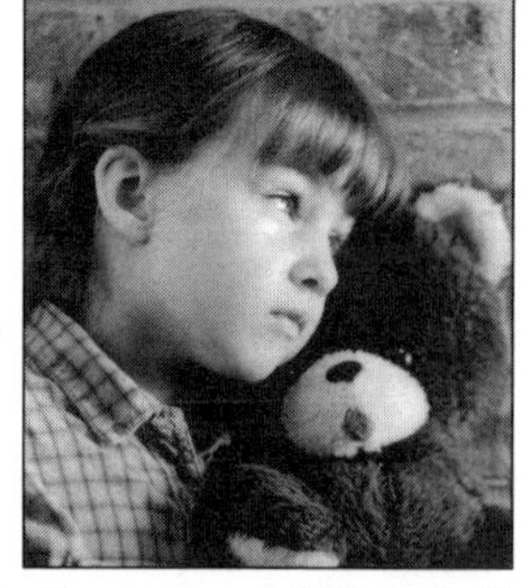

A typical consequence of child abuse is a loss of trust. This loss of trust generally extends to adults other than the abuser. The child's relationship with members of his family suffers. Without trust, relationships within the family are shaken. It is possible that some relationships will never be restored without supernatural intervention.

Abused children often have difficulties socially. Fear and a lack of security contribute to this. Abused children tend to have a lower self-esteem than they would otherwise. Some retreat into shyness and become extremely introverted.

One of the saddest aspects of abuse is its self-perpetuating nature. Although it seems odd, an abused child often grows up to be an abuser. It is not that the abused wants revenge for hurts experienced. Rather, the abused repeats patterns which have been modeled by significant individuals in his life.

9. First Kings 15:1-3,26,33,34; 16:1,2,15-20 record the reigns of a series of kings of Israel. What did each of these kings have in common and how does this illustrate the self-perpetuating nature of sin from generation to generation?

____

____

As abused children approach adolescence, like other children, they will begin experiencing interest in the opposite sex. Unfortunately, if they have been sexually abused, it may affect how they deal with these new feelings. Many will react in either of two extremes. One extreme is to become extremely introverted which results in not having to deal with the opposite sex whenever possible. The other extreme is becoming promiscuous, looking for love, affection, and acceptance in all the wrong places.

The Abuser

The abuser also pays a price for his actions. Caught in a trap of horrid behavior, many abusers are torn between the feelings of power and control over their victim and the realization that what they are doing is terribly wrong. Secretly, many abusers wish to be caught in order to end their tragic behavior.

Legal ramifications await the more grievous offenders. Courts often administer the strictest punishments allowed by law against child abusers. Unfortunately, there is little successful rehabilitation within the justice system. Many abusers return to society and repeat their crimes.

10. Look at Romans 13:2-4. What is the role of the justice system in dealing with child abusers? By what authority?

____

____

____

Churches must be careful in ministering to the child abuser. Offering an abuser full restoration too quickly can place a defenseless child at risk. Withholding forgiveness to the truly repentant can destroy the individual. As repulsive as child abuse is, it must be remembered that God not only agonizes for the abused child, but also for the perpetrator. As difficult as it is, as Christians, we need to remember that fact.

11. Compare 1 Corinthians 5:1-13 with 2 Corinthians 2:5-11. What does Paul teach about the church's responsibility toward blatant sin and the sinner?

____

____

____

The Family

The pain of child abuse is not limited to the child. The child's family also experiences a great sense of pain, anger, and loss. They may feel guilt, helplessness (why couldn't I protect my child from this awful crime?), and shame (how can we deal with the humiliation and disgrace?). The family unit is altered, never to be exactly as it was before.

Members of the child's family may find their sense of trust toward others (even God) weakened. Becoming involved with social events and activities may be more difficult; family members may regard others suspiciously. If the abuser was a family member, many of these feelings and attitudes may be intensified.

12. According to Revelation 12:10, what is one of Satan's daily activities? How does Satan use this same technique against innocent family members in an abusive situation?

____

____

____

____

____

HEALING THE HURT

Healing For The Child

The wounds children suffer at the hands of an abuser are deep. Only those who have endured the pain can fully comprehend the full ramifications. One wonders, *How can these victims be healed and restored?*

Therapy and counseling can help the child gain perspective and deal with the situation. However, more than therapy is needed for a complete recovery.

God is a compassionate, loving God. Only He can provide the comfort, restoration, and healing needed by the abused child. There may be hurdles for the child to overcome before he is able to accept the love and comfort of God. A lack of trust in any authority figure may hinder his positive response. Another hurdle will present itself if the abuser was a father figure. For many, looking past the characteristics of the abusive father to the loving nature of his Heavenly Father is monumental. However, as the abused child learns more about the love, sacrifice, and unconditional acceptance of God, he will accept salvation and find inner healing. The child who has been abused must be approached with the gospel gently, with love and patience.

After the child accepts Jesus as Savior, he needs teaching. It is important that the child continues learning about the love, mercy, and healing power of the Lord. As the child learns more about the nature of God, he can approach the Lord with his needs and allow the healing process to continue.

As the child receives healing from God, he can better accept himself. It is important that adults help him see the abuse was not his fault and he is not to blame for the situation. The past and future must be committed to the Lord. With anticipation, the child should be taught to look forward to God's healing touch. This doesn't mean that the past or the pain the child feels should be ignored. It does mean that the child is directed to find his healing in the Lord.

Becoming reconciled to others will take time, as will healthy, positive experiences. Some children will have no problem trusting those who stood by them, never violating their trust. Others will develop fears and reservations towards everyone. Most abused children will regard new acquaintances with reservation and even suspicion. Common gestures, such as hugs or handshakes, may be uncomfortable for them. Adults must be sensitive to their feelings and work with the children to reestablish trust and confidence in people. Learning about the love of God, and being in a warm fellowship of believers, provides them with opportunities to reconcile with others.

13. **Read 2 Corinthians 1:3-11. How could this Scripture help a child who had suffered abuse?**

____

____

____

Healing For The Abuser

In crimes against children, it is sometimes easy to forget the offender as we concentrate on the one abused. However, the abuser is in need of healing, forgiveness, and restoration.

14. **According to Galatians 6:1-5, what is the spiritual responsibility to a truly repentant sinner?**

____

____

It could be easy to assume the sin of child abuse is beyond forgiveness. But, thank God, that is not true. There is nothing our God can't reach and forgive. The perpetrator may need God's help in forgiving himself, and others may as well. However, God is always ready and eager to forgive anyone who is truly repentant.

Healing For The Family

Child abuse causes pain and suffering for all involved. The child's family is hurt. The sense of loss and the agony of not being able to protect their child may seem to haunt family members. They too, need healing and restoration.

God's healing power is not limited to physical wounds and is not just for the victim. God can closely identify with the agony parents feel, as His own Son suffered abuse at the hands of others. He is willing and able to heal and unify the family, emotionally and spiritually.

SUMMARY

Child abuse is one of the most tragic crimes that can occur. The physical pain and emotional suffering can only be fully understood by those who have endured it. The wounds suffered at the hands of an abuser are neither quickly forgotten nor easily healed.

Child abuse can be avoided. One of the first steps in stopping child abuse is to admit that it exists. Adults also need to admit that raising a child is a difficult job. Gaining as much understanding as possible concerning child development and children's needs will help parents prepare themselves for the inevitable times of stress.

When abuse does occur, therapy and counseling can be helpful for the victim, the offender, and also their families. It must be remembered, however, Christians have a resource which far surpasses psychological techniques. Jesus Christ can provide healing which surpasses understanding.

LET'S REVIEW

1. Name and describe four different types of child abuse.

2. What are the consequences of child abuse for the child? for the abuser?

3. What are some things parents can do to protect their children from child abuse?

4. How can an abused child experience healing?